THE CIPHER OF GENESIS

"Suarès goes back to the original Hebrew 'number-letters' in which the Old Testament was written, removes myths and stories that resulted from mere translation of words, and presents a psychological experience that is not historical but is evolving for each one now."

—*San Francisco Chronicle*

THE CIPHER
OF GENESIS

The Original Code of the
Qabala as Applied to the Scriptures

Carlo Suarès

SAMUEL WEISER, INC.

York Beach, Maine

First published in 1992 by
Samuel Weiser, Inc.
P. O. Box 612
York Beach, Maine 03910-0612
www.weiserbooks.com

This edition published by arrangement with Shambhala Publications, Inc.

09 08 07 06 05 04 03 02 01 00
14 13 12 11 10 9   8   7   6   5

Library of Congress Cataloging-in-Publication Data
Suarès, Carlo.
    [Bible restitutée. English]
    The cipher of Genesis: the original code of the Qabala as applied to the
    Scriptures / by Carlo Suarès
    p.   cm.
    Translation of : La Bible restituée
    Originally published: Berkeley: Shambhala Publications, 1970, in series:
Clear light series.
    Includes index.
    1. Bible. O. T. Genesis—Miscellenea. 2. Cabala. 3. Gematria.
I. Title
BS1235.5.2813   1992   91-40972
222'.11068—dc20   CIP
ISBN 0-87728-740-6
BJ

Printed in the United States of America

The paper used in this publication meets the minimum requirements of the
American National Standard for Information Science—Permanence of Paper
for Printed Library Materials Z39.48-1992(R1997).

Contents

CONTENTS

PART THREE
THE GOSPELS

The manuscript has been read and commented upon (in succession) by the following and has benefited by their suggestions and revisions:

Nadine Suarès, Eleanor Foster, Mary Shannon, Ferris and Iris Hartman, George Buchanan, Anne Lindbergh, Humphrey Noyes, Ernest Dale

In acknowledgment and deep gratitude, C.S.

"The heavens themselves, the planets and this centre
Observe degree, priority, and place,
Insisture, course, proportion, season, form,
Office, and custom, in all line of order."
Troilus and Cressida Act 1, Sc. iii

Foreword

CARLO SUARÈS dedicated a great part of his life to unravelling the revelatory meanings hidden in the code of the Bible. It was, in fact, forty years before the transcendent truths of the Bible yielded to his patient perseverance and his unshakable conviction that the original version read in letter-numbers of the Hebrew alphabet contained the secret of man's transfiguration.

Humphrey Noyes

Introduction

NOT VERY long ago artificial institutions and moral values were the terms for our civilization. Such definitions have gradually revealed their inadequacy in every sphere in the rapidly changing circumstances of our world, and an articulate call for the rediscovery of the sacred fount which is believed to exist in our Scriptures is heard everywhere.

Our many-sided sciences make almost daily discoveries—or inventions—of collaterals which by mere impact of observation acquire the status of distinct branches, thereby splitting further our already scattered body of knowledge. In spite of the increasing hold of mathematics on departments as far apart as optics, philology, biology or ethics, it cannot and will never discover a basic postulate befitting the simultaneous existence of a universe and of man.

Some religiously-minded people are aware of this lack of a unitary way of thought capable of including the knowledge of man and the knowledge of things. Although far too late, they are only just in time to measure, not without some perplexity, the unthought-of distance which separates them from the world as it is.

Like bewildered passengers in a ship astray on uncharted seas, whose call to Saviours is of no avail, we are told to believe in a brotherly huddle, to feed the hungry and clothe the naked as a means of atonement.

Does not the sacred thus humanized fall under Jesus' curse: *Get thee behind me, Satan: thou art an offence to me: for thou savourest not the things that be of God, but those that be of men* (Matt. xvi, 23)?

This emphasizing of "the things that be of man" stressed by

11

so many churches today—in an attempt to recapture their grip on human affairs—blended with a clinging to obsolete myths does not lead to the sacred fount of revelation and knowledge, but rather to an alienation from it. In order to obviate this estrangement, high authorities have asked learned personalities, priests, monks, ministers, rabbis, to co-operate in retranslating the Bible into different languages. In this connection the most ancient of ancient traditions (the Qabala) cannot but issue a severe warning to those scholars: their monumental task will not lead them any nearer the Source, not only because the Bible is untranslatable but, strange as it may seem, because it is already hopelessly mistranslated in Hebrew.

*

The twenty-two graphs which are used as letters in the Hebrew alphabet are twenty-two proper names originally used to designate different states or structures of the one cosmic energy, which is *essence* and *semblance*, of all that is. Even though they correspond to numbers, symbols and ideas, those twenty-two vastly exceed all the most exhaustive sets of classes: they cannot be distributed among things because they factually *are* that which they designate.

One has to probe very deeply into this semasiology to realize that this last statement does not exceed the limits of truth and need not be a cause of astonishment. We are approaching here a language which is not a by-product of sensorial references, but a would-be transmission from the unknown. Hence the difficulty of explaining it, because of the inability of the human mind to grasp that which is not contained in a frame of recognition.

This present essay is, however, an attempt to overcome that difficulty by suggesting a number of approaches, which, it is hoped, will gradually uncover that which is purported to be rediscovered: the secret and sacred fount lying in the hidden depths of the Bible.

A direct approach would be to introduce immediately the

code with which to decipher the Bible, and to begin with the first schemata of the Genesis: *Bereschyt Barah Elohim* . . . etc. . . . but it is doubtful whether the readers would willingly follow such a plan, without first having found a good reason for so doing. The statement that the twenty-two letters of the Hebrew alphabet are but the initials of names, the meanings of which have been lost throughout the ages, gives rise to such legitimate questions as to *how, whence*, and *why*.

The *why* is simply the fact that the Book of Genesis was originally a cabalistic script. The *whence* is lost in immemorial time, through centuries of history, proto-history, pseudo-history, myths and legends. The *how* is a secretly transmitted tradition the thread of which was never lost and which for many reasons has remained hidden. But things have come to such a point, in our present juncture of historical and psychological events, when it is necessary that it should be revealed, by bestowing its basic key: the code of those names which have been desecrated to the point of being made use of in an alphabet constituted by only their initials. (Whereas our A, B, C, and so on, are mere representations of vocal sounds, the names Aleph, Bayt, Ghimel, etc. are projections of biologically structured energies in different stages of organization.)

The decoding of Genesis and of any other cabalistic text is therefore not a mere matter of transposing from A-B-C to Aleph-Bayt-Ghimel, but a process of penetrating an unknown world by means of a manner of thinking which has to be experienced by the very use of the language which must be learned in order to understand it. However paradoxical and perhaps difficult this may appear, it stands to reason that were the Revelation a matter of ordinary words, it would be an obvious fact prone to superficial observation.

The words we use in our languages are conventional. They do not emanate from the objects which they designate. The word *house* is understood just as well as *maison* in French or *casa* in Italian: none of those words has any ontological link with the essence of the object thus specified, and their use merely helps us to recognize such objects, by means of linguistic agreements.

We come to realize that the problem of conveying the unknown could only be solved if it were possible to project the common essence of everything which is in the universe as a whole (including, of course, Man, because the essence is One). That essence in Man is according to cabalistic postulates a movement both inner and outer, which builds structures and destroys them unceasingly. Our psychological inner structures built with and upon words which never convey the things, but are our ideas of what we recognize their appearances to be, must therefore be atomized, so to speak, in order for us to partake in and commune with the cosmic unfathomable mystery of the one movement, which is life.

There will never be any explanation of why anything exists at all. The dogmas of the beginning of a Creation and a God who creates will never be anything but futile attempts to explain away the mystery which is the totality of time and space and life and, in a word: of being. On that assertion is founded the Qabala.

The Qabala—which among thousands of scripts, includes Genesis and scattered fragments of other biblical sources— stands unremittingly against every projection of thought concerning the essence of life, because projections are but images, symbols and vagrant words. Qabala existed even before Abraham and therefore does not belong to any specific tradition. It is not—as so repeatedly stated by so-called experts—a mysticism or any mysterious system of occultism. It is a way of thinking based on unitive postulates and analogical developments, of which our modern thought can well take advantage. For many centuries it has been the nutritive roots of our civilizations, hidden in the gnostic teachings and in many schools of thought. Whether deliberately ignored or criticized with blatant prejudice, whether feared or laughed at, this vital knowledge and its subdivisions of structures has always been misunderstood. The reason for such constant ostracism will appear only too clearly when this essay is subjected to the criticism of Tradition founded on ecclesiasticism. In spite, however, or *because* of the assertion that the Bible has been, for centuries, and still is being read in a sense contrary to its intent, we trust religious as well as scientific circles to respond to it with interest.

PART ONE

HA-QABALA

Ha-Qabala

FREQUENTLY, OVER the centuries, the Qabala has been lost and rediscovered. Its traces can be found in the period when, back from their captivity in Babylon, the Jews awoke to a new awareness of themselves, with Ezra, Nehemiah and others.

Looking backwards in time, we can see that the Qabala was alive with Mosheh (Moses); going back further, we find it with Abram; in still more remote ages, it disappears from the sight of enquirers, but not from the perception of those who have inherited that most ancient of ancient knowledge. All through history its transmission has been kept secret. The source of the original Qabala can, however, be grasped at any time, because it is timeless. The cabalists have always said that Abram possessed it.

Ab-Ram (the father of Ram, or according to the Semitic expression, "he who possesses" Ram) may have been an initiate of any country from Tibet to Egypt. In Tibet the name Ram expresses the universal essence, in the sense of "basis of the world", and is also sometimes a symbol of all that radiates as the sun. Ram, in ancient Egypt, was also a symbol for the basis of the world, manifested in the pyramids (in Arabic pyramid is Ahram). One of the most important persons in the Egyptian initiatic order was Ram Nak Hotep.

The name Ram is also linked to the Celtic world where, for the Druids, it was the symbol of the universal essence. It was said that those who had pierced the secret of Ram could disregard all the unessentials, retaining only the essential.

In the English sense, "ram", the animal, is found as a symbol in the esoteric teaching of the Prajna-Patis (lords of the Being);

it pierces through all that is not essential. Its motto is: "Let us be gods and laugh at ourselves."

According to the original Qabala, Ram expresses the "cosmic dwelling", that is, the whole perceptible extant universe in its capacity for proliferation. And Avram, or Abram, is he who, having gone through the many layers of differentiation, receives the pulsation of life which transfigures that proliferation on a level with cosmic action. In simple words, the action of an Avram in his own house has a cosmic significance.

Abraham was not a believer. He recognized the presence of life as an ally and made with it a covenant. That pact was two-fold: it included (a) the Qabala, that is, a direct penetration of knowledge through comprehension, examination, vision and writing, and (b) circumcision on the eighth day, that is, direct penetration of vital energy, transmutation of animal sexuality for the benefit of a sensitivity of the entire nervous system awakened and alert.

A few pages will later be devoted to circumcision, one of the keys to the mystery of Israel. I say that there are two keys. One is for the body, the sensory apparatus, the psyche: the circumcision on the eighth day. The other is for the mind, the contained, the human and cosmic germ of life unconditioned, which can only "be" when it is indeterminate: the Qabala.

★

Abram possessed the Qabala as knowledge and as writing. It has been said that the document whereon was inscribed the number-code of that knowledge came from Mount Ararat, where the mythical Noah's Ark had come to rest after the Deluge. Ararat, according to an ancient tradition, is the cabalistic name for a new cycle which comes into being after a long period during which the human germ has not been able to develop. Ararat means that two worlds, the timeless and the measurable (the inner and the outer) were again ready to make a fresh start. They were close together but not in any way related because the earlier human bodies still belonged to the primitive female.

Noah's consciousness, absorbed by the wine which the female earth had engendered, had sunk to a low level. The human germ in evolution had been transferred to Shem, the eponymic ancestor of the Semites. We must here pass over Shem's ten symbolic generations and come to old Terahh, Abram's father. Their marvellous story will be told in its proper place, but we wish now to mention the place of Abram's birth: Aur Kasdeem, translated Ur of the Chaldees. Symbolically, according to the Qabala, it means: the light of the magicians. Aur in Hebrew means light, and the Kasdeems are the magicians, astrologers, diviners, who exercised great influence in those times.

The cabalists have always had a horror of the magic of the Kasdeems. Abram is the beginning of yet another era. With him, religion begins to free itself from the "light of the magicians", and to direct itself towards the perception of the inner light of YHWH. In Abram's hand is a marvellous document: the testament of a lost civilization, brought in the ark.

A few survivors had been able to preserve, in a series of ideograms, all that men had ever known, all that men will ever know, concerning the vocation of mankind in the presence of the impenetrable mystery of being.

Of these survivors, Genesis says (VI, 4) that *the sons of Elohim came in unto the daughters of men, and they bare children to them*. In the time of Shem, they had disappeared from memory, but they had bequeathed their knowledge orally and had entrusted their precious document to safe hands.

According to the esoteric tradition, Abram was the first really to understand the deep significance of their message. The human seed had to disentangle itself from the magic of the Kasdeem where it was being held in bondage, and had to be thrust into the world of conflict, of uncertainty, of hope and utter despair, of wild joy and anguish, of obstinate reconstructions and impending disasters. Any refuge, any protecting shelter had to be denied to it because, were it ever to remain immobile in any peaceful surrounding, it would become static in an immature, pre-human sub-species.

That land of strife and joys and pain is called, symbolically, Canaan. Abram was sent into that land to take root and to conquer.

The biblical narrative, from there on, is a vast epic poem where all the themes of the myth reappear in a common adventure through such names as Abraham and Sarah, Isaac and Rebecca, Jacob, Leah, Rachel, Esau, etc.

The subject of that epic poem is the description of the implanting of the human seed in the symbolical Canaan, or, on another level, it shows how duality is conquered by the three-fold movement of life, in humanity-to-be.

Abram becomes Abraham, and he transmits the Qabala to his son Isaac. Isaac gives it eventually to Jacob; and Jacob, disappointed by most of his sons, chooses as the heir to that knowledge his eleventh son, Yosseph (Joseph). The way in which he makes his choice is to send him in to an ambush planned by Yosseph's brothers with the purpose of killing him.

The attempted murder of the elected one is in the purest Yahwic style. In the beginning of the myth, YHWH had become incarnate in his son Cain, and the simple presence of the timeless and indeterminate Cain had been enough to burst the bag of blood called Abel.

Of course, Cain had not killed him: Abel had fallen into the non-entity of his own conditioning, and the earth had drunk his blood. Abel cannot be reproached for being dull as are all the people who work and sweat and merely exist in their mediocrity. In him, the seed of humanity-to-be could not live.

Aware of this result, YHWH became cautious and decided to submit to a test the people he planned to utilize: he would try to kill them. If they resisted, they would be strong enough to carry the seed. Thus he commanded Abraham to kill Isaac. Elohim assaulted Jacob and wrestled with him a whole night. He deceived Moses so as to attack him unawares. (Exod. x, 1-27) YHWH says to Moses, *Go in unto Pharaoh for I have hardened his heart.* (Logically he would have helped Moses had he softened Pharaoh's heart.) YHWH *hardened Pharaoh's heart and he would not let them* (the Hebrews) *go.* (Exod. IV, 19 and 24) *And YHWH said unto Moses in Midian, Go, return into Egypt, for all the men are dead which sought thy life,* . . . and when Moses is thus lulled, YHWH attempts to kill him.

In this passage (as well as in those that follow) we can see an example of the ''personalization process' which inevitably occurs when these texts are read without a previous knowledge of the code which relates to their symbols. According to this manner of thinking it is, to be sure, quite evident that the cosmic vocation of Man—Adam—is to permit the two lives that make up his own double life to fecundate one another, mutually. He will thus become a new being and the actualization of the immanence, YHWH, will take place within him.

And it is of such manifestation, with its ensuing transformations, that the cabalists speak when they seem to attribute speech and action to the YHWH immanence, whose acts and words are to be found, for them, on a purely symbolic level. Further, many characters referred to in these stories (Cain, Abel, Lemekh, Noah) are mythical archetypes and should not, in any circumstances, be considered as being historical persons.

But let us return to Joseph, ''sold by his brothers''. That episode is a distorted description of an initiatic ceremony. Some of its elements are significant: Joseph was in a state of half-dream: he was stripped *of his coat, his coat of many colours that was on him* (Gen. XXXVII, 23-28). This is a wrong translation. His robe was the robe of spoliation (or dispossession); *he was cast into a pit: and the pit was empty, there was no water in it.* And Yehoudah (Judah) suggested, *let us* sell him, and he was sold for *20 pieces of silver.*

All these symbols are clear to those who know the Qabala.

The mythical Joseph is a dual entity. Being the eleventh son, he is both 10, which is the number of Yod, and 1, the Aleph. The Aleph allowed him to understand dreams, and the Yod gave him the capacity to purchase all the wheat of Egypt.

In very truth, Joseph's action was the very action of the myth. He was a man of the Qabala when he came to Egypt. He was a conjunction of two processes: myth and history. He was that which a few initiates in the Qabala happen to be from time to time: the historical consciousness of the myth's biological necessity. A necessity which, more often than not, has appeared under the aspect of some devastating punishment inflicted by YHWH.

Joseph brought upon his people a substantial blessing, which was immediately followed by a threat of wholesale destruction, by utter misery, by a most difficult escape, and by endless hardships. He was ambivalent. The myth is male, the earthly possessions are female.

Joseph kneaded and molded the primitive, formless substance of the human masses. He crushed them powerfully so as to compel them to react vitally.

Before his time, human Genesis was (mythically) concentrated in a family. With him was born a people, a nation.

This is how YHWH operated: there was a famine in Mitzrayim (Egypt) and in all adjoining countries. This Joseph had foreseen and he purchased for Pharaoh every grain of wheat available in the whole of Egypt. He then agreed to distribute it, but only at the price of dispossession. Thus, as a result of the operation, Pharaoh was the possessor of every acre in Egypt, and the whole people were reduced to slavery.

In the meanwhile, Joseph had asked all his family to come, and had settled them on the best land of the country so that they might multiply exceedingly.

Throughout there are two incidents which reveal to the cabalist that Joseph inherited the Qabala. In Genesis XLVII, 29, we learn that when Joseph's father, Jacob, whose real name is Israel, was about to die, he said to Joseph, *Put, I pray thee, thy hand under my thigh, and deal kindly with me.* We remember (Gen. XXXII, 25) that after having wrestled with Jacob all night, Elohim *prevailed not against him,* and wounded him in *the hollow of his thigh.*

The fact of asking Joseph to touch that consecrated wound has a very profound, symbolic meaning. An ever present mythical idea is that "he who heals must be wounded", "he who is life must have gone through death". Israel, in this episode, transfers his power to Joseph by revealing himself to him.

Another verse is Genesis XLIII, 22, in which Israel says to Joseph: *Moreover, I have given to thee one portion above thy brethren, which I took out of the hand of the Amorite with my sword and with my bow.*

The Amorite, the sword and the bow are very hard indeed to interpret! Israel never held a sword or a bow in his hands, and never fought anyone except Elohim. This is a somewhat amusing case of mistranslation, due to the rational logic of translators who, in their ignorance, could not allow themselves to believe that Israel was mentioning *the hand that had talked to him.*

The root Amer, or Homer, which is used in the original text, is a reference to speech and has become "an Amorite". A Hand that speaks is a hand that writes. The object bequeathed, about which the exegesis knows nothing, is well known esoterically. It is none other than the secret document, the trace of which is seen here.

Joseph lived a life of pomp and power. He died and was embalmed after the manner of the great of this world.

After his death, the Egyptian priests sought to find the magic object—or document—which Israel had given to his son, but they failed to do so. It had disappeared, and nobody knew where it was. Thus, many years passed by.

Then came a time when (Exod. I, 8-14) *there arose up a new king over Egypt, which knew not Joseph.* Because of the tremendous power which the throne and the hierarchy had received from Joseph, the people were more and more miserable. But also because of Joseph, *the children of Israel were fruitful and increasea abundantly.* The more they were afflicted, *the more they multiplied and grew.* They became *numerous and more powerful* than the Egyptians. The harder their lives, the more bitter with bondage they became, the stronger they grew. Pharaoh decided to exterminate them. He ordered the Hebrew midwives to kill the new-born sons. They disobeyed in full agreement with Elohim; the babies were saved; and now we come to the story of **Moses**, and we shall rediscover the lost Qabala in an unexpected place.

The story of Moses—we prefer to use his real name Mosheh— is, in the beginning, similar to many other legends of new-born children threatened, hidden, found, saved and led towards an exalted mission.

Much has been written on Mosheh, from different points of view, but it seems to me that only the Qabala can see him in his double reality, which is both mythical and historical.

The mythical reality is the evolution throughout the ages of the relationship between human consciousness and the unfathomable mystery of existence, resulting from the laws of Moses.

We have already stated that in the perception of the fact that existence is a total mystery lies the foundation of any true religious awareness. The mystery, the realization that the fact of existence cannot be explained in words or in any other way, has always been deeply alive in the minds of the men of the Qabala.

This does not mean that their writings correspond adequately to the needs of our time.

If they said in symbols what can be set forth today clearly in words, it is because it was thus that they understood and felt. But when we want to understand and feel, we must break through those images and expressions which served them, but which no longer serve. We do not see Abraham or Mosheh as did the ancient cabalists. We see them with our own eyes and judgment. We can and must see them directly. We can penetrate their legendary existences, and so discern that they were not what they are said to have been. We can do this because the historical process functions on a certain sensorial level, whereas the mythical process concerns the psyche, and, whether yesterday or today, the Qabala is always in touch, through the psyche with the great unknown.

26

At certain particularly important conjunctions of this double process, the Hebrew myth becomes apparent and thrusts itself upon the objective world where it acts as a typhoon whose whirling motion draws waters from the ocean and carries them along with its own movement. The mass of waters thus captured belongs more to the cyclone than to the ocean.

Such events as those which are named Abraham, Mosheh or Jesus are thus taken over by the myth and belong to it more than they do to objective reality. Their immense importance is due to the fact that they are a conjunction of two realities. Finally, they modify the course of history in so far as they become religious phenomena.

Certain Asiatic myths carry through centuries the continuity of their religious and social structures. They can be compared to very old trees of knowledge whose fruits have dried on their branches for lack of any renewed sap. Contrarily, the Qabala has died and has resurrected many, many times amidst spectacular displays, on each occasion accomplishing and then burying its past.

If, by chance, we happen today to be in such a time, we are the very conjunction, the very timeless spark, which at one time appeared as Abraham, at another time as Mosheh, and later as Jesus. That pinpoint of recurrent eternity is the Qabala.

These considerations will be useful, we believe, now that we are about to resume our exploration of the narrative concerning Mosheh. Joseph had long been dead, and the Qabala had disappeared: both Joseph and the Qabala were completely forgotten, and the people were in utter misery.

With Mosheh springing out of the waters, a new birth on an entirely different level takes place, both identical and opposite to that which had been prepared by YHWH through Joseph.

We are compelled here, although not without some reluctance, to recall a terminology rather well known to the Qabala and to say that with Mosheh the narrative of the Emanation is now over and opens into the Creation, then into the Formation and the Action of Israel.

We said that the epoch of single men who carried the seed of human perfection has given place, with Joseph, to an epoch where that seed had to be buried in very primitive people. The tribes were 70 persons on their arrival in Egypt. But 430 years had elapsed and at the time of the Exodus, they were, according to the texts, 600,000 men, not including the children and without mentioning the women.

The problem was how to preserve the Elohimic seed, buried deep in a primitive, coarse, brutal human substance, hopelessly incapable of deconditioning itself.

The Qabala uses the word Sephiroth to express or describe different structures of the *one* cosmic energy, the Ayn-Soph. Their formulation, in the time of Mosheh, was beyond the understanding of the unevolved masses. The creative energy was bound to be deeply involved and immersed in blood.

The Sephiroth, or cosmic energies, which had operated in emanation through the myth, from Adam up to Abraham and his family, degenerated into other Sephiroth. Intelligence became Rigour, and Wisdom became Clemency, according to the Qabala.

The book of Mosheh, in fact, opens on those two key notes. This book is the book of a Creation. It is the creation of a container, of a living garment of protection for the seed of humanity-to-be, capable of not only sheltering it but also of living in symbiosis with it, of being in at-one-ment with it, until the time of the necessary ripening and ultimate destruction of the shell.

Because the times are ripe today, the entire process of birth, growth, maturity, old age and death of the myth appears to us very clearly.

The two Sephiroth, Rigour and Clemency, accompany the action of Mosheh-Aaron. The two keys to the mystery of Israel, circumcision and the knowledge of the Name, are given to Mosheh. It is a new departure and the beginning of a very long story, which lies outside the scope of the present essay. We must, however, include this story and the new expression of the Qabala as we give it in the general field of the occult tradition.

We will, therefore, give a short account of the legend of Mosheh as seen from the angle of this Qabala.

Mosheh is spelled Mem-Sheen-Hay. The Mem stands for water (as originator of existence), the Sheen symbolizes the Cosmic breath, and Hay means life. During a given liftetime, when the immense Exodus was being prepared, we can well imagine what such a revolt and such a devastating decision must have meant for the people. They had to be stirred and literally doped by miraculous messages, predictions, promises. They had to believe in something tremendous. A vigorous and active deity was needed: the need was fulfilled.

The myth, like a cyclone, fell upon them with such intensity that with the help of their heated imaginations, tremendous happenings were supposed to take place, such as the ten plagues of Egypt, when one half of any one of them would have been enough to destroy the whole country.

The most interesting part of it is the quarrel between YHWH and Pharaoh, each threatening to kill the other's first-born.* When YHWH thus threatens Pharaoh, he sets about, without wasting a minute, to try to kill his own son. (Exod. IV, 22-24) says YHWH to Mosheh: *And thou shalt say unto Pharaoh, thus saith YHWH, Israel is my son, my first-born. And I say unto thee, let my son go that he may serve me, and if thou refuse to let him go, I will slay thy son, thy first-born. And it came to pass in a place where he spent the night that YHWH met him* (Mosheh) *and sought to kill him.*

The conflict is intensified. Pharaoh oppresses the people more and more. YHWH sends all his plagues and as Pharaoh does not yield, comes to a last dramatic decision: all the new-born of Egypt are to be slaughtered.

The dispute between YHWH and the Earth (or the earthly powers) as to whose son is the first-born and what is to became of him is recurrent in the Bible, and—according to the Qabala

---

* Here, and in the following pages, we make use of the language of the Bible, which, as has already been said, personalizes YHWH, in order to render the term intelligible.

—is of vital importance for everyone of us. We shall deal with it at some length in subsequent chapters.

Another subject of dispute is "blood". This symbol has a wide range of connotations. The first plague inflicted by YHWH upon Egypt is the changing of all the water into blood. The Egyptian magicians can do it, too. Eventually Jesus will change water into wine. Blood and wine are interchangeable symbols. From Jesus' wounds it is said that the blood was mixed with water.

The night before the Exodus, the Hebrews stained their doors with blood so as to be recognized by the slaughterers and spared.

The Qabala insists on the significance of the name Adam: "dam" in Hebrew means blood. Within it is the hidden Aleph.

Another important symbol in Mosheh's story is the transfiguration of womanhood. We shall follow this essential theme all through Genesis and as far as the Gospels. It is always through woman that every step from Emanation to Creation to Formation and to Action is achieved. In Mosheh's narrative, two midwives, in agreement with Elohim, save YHWH's first-born. Mosheh is saved a second time by two women, one of them being his sister. (The symbol "sister" will be explained at length in connection with Sarah, Rebecca and Rachel.)

One of the first episodes concerning Mosheh is when he sees an Egyptian and a Hebrew fighting. He kills the Egyptian (Harshness). He is very much afraid lest he be discovered and punished. He digs a hole in the sand and buries the body. Then he meets two Hebrews fighting and wants to intervene as he has done previously. They ask him, "Do you wish to kill us as you killed the Egyptian?" Mosheh thus realizing that his deed is known, decides to flee and save himself (Clemency).

Mosheh is therefore compelled to go to Midian, towards his destiny. The "Cohen" (priest) of Midian has 7 symbolic daughters. Mosheh meets them at a well and delivers them out of the hands of some shepherds. The daughters go to their father, whose name is Reuel (Exod. ii, 20), *and he said unto his daughters, And where is he? Why is it that you have left the man? Cal him that he may eat bread.*

Mosheh eventually marries one of the 7 sisters. Her name is Zifforah.

Now begins chapter III thus: *Now Moses kept the flock of Jethro his father-in-law.* Very few readers observe that the man whose name was Reuel is now named Jethro. But the Qabala knows why this is so and how it happened.

When Israel died, his sons took his body and carried it all the way to Mamreh, to bury it. With them they carried the precious Qabala to save it from the Egyptians, and gave it in trust in Midian to some descendants of Abraham.

The mythical Reuel is clearly said to be (according to his name) Elohim's shepherd. Informed by his symbolic 7 daughters about the man who "delivered" them, he understands that, after so many years of waiting, he that was to be the inheritor of the Qabala has at last come.

The name Zifforah is again a symbol. She could be the princess Aurora of a fairy tale. Her name is the call of morning, a rising, a departure.

Reuel, having transmitted his powers to Mosheh, becomes somebody else: a sheer existence deeply immersed in its resistance to life-death. He falls, so to speak, into a coarser layer of vibrations, following the sephirotic process of incarnation. His part, as we shall soon see, will prevail in the creation of a tribal deity. So he is no longer Reuel, he now is Jethro.

Mosheh is aware of his future mission. He will serve YHWH, but so far he has not a direct revelation of what YHWH is. He is a stranger to that name, so he calls his son Gershon, which means stranger.

One day he goes with Jethro's flocks beyond the lands he usually treads. He goes into the enchanted regions of Elohim's desolate life, into the deep dwellings of existence. That region has a name: Horeb. From its terrible dryness, a spark of light flashes suddenly, an "angel", *and, behold, the bush burned with fire, and the bush was not consumed* (Exod. III, 2).

YHWH sees that Mosheh turns round *to see this great light,* and to wonder *why this bush is not burnt.* Then comes the revelation.

Mosheh's mission is now fully revealed to him, but he still does not know whose voice it is that speaks to him. (Exod. III, 13) *When I come unto the children of Israel . . . and they shall say to me, what is his name? what shall I say unto them?* And here come the prodigious revelation, the splendid, the dazzling truth: "*Aleph-Hay-Yod-Hay. Aleph-Sheen-Raysh. Aleph-Hay-Yod-Hay.*"

All the translations of these ideograms, even in the Hebrew language, are abominable desecrations. A man skilled in the Qabala needs but to contemplate those few signs to be aware of it. If he truly is of the Qabala, the universe invades him with all that lives and all that dies, and that which exists, and that which does not exist, and that which has ever existed, and that which will be, and that which never was; though time and space are there, they dissolve into timelessness; for therein lies the prodigious mystery of all that is determined by indetermination. The sanctification is there, and a man dies to himself for being so much alive.

It is thus said: Go and say: *Aleph-Hay-Yod-Hay has sent me to you.* Yes. *You will say Yod-Hay-Vav-Hay has sent me to you.* Yes. Aleph-Hay-Yod-Hay. Yes. Yod-Hay-Vav-Hay. A Yod for an Aleph. A Hay for a Yod. A Vav for a Yod. A Hay for a Hay.

And that is the Qabala. It is easy to understand it when one knows the game, the game that the Aleph-life-death-life-death and the Yod-existence must play continuously; the Aleph, discontinuous pulsation, at times immanent, at times activated, and Yod permanent and continuous: Yod the perpetual loser in spite of the psyche that does not want to die. All this is easy to understand when one knows that all life is two lives and that Adam is Aleph inside the blood.

Such is the revelation granted to Mosheh of one of the two mysteries of Israel: the Qabala. The other mystery is the circumcision. It will be granted, as we all know, by Zifforah, when she will save Mosheh from YHWH's aggression (Exod. IV,

25-26): *Then Zifforah took a sharp stone and cut off the foreskin of her son and cast it at his feet, and said, Surely a bloody husband art thou to me. So he let him go: then she said, A bloody husband thou art, because of the circumcision.*

If we imagine YHWH as a tramp or a brigand at large, and fail to understand the truth underlying those symbols, this episode appears to be insane. When we know the inner, vital necessity of the myth, YHWH, Zipporah and Mosheh himself are only personifications of symbols.

The objective historical fact is that from that time on, a covenant has been established between YHWH and Israel in its flesh and life evolving towards a higher state of humanity. The movement of that life is integrated in the bodies of flesh, whether the Jews yield to it or not.

Many tentative explanations have been given of how the Hebrews crossed the Red Sea, of how Mosheh struck water out of a dry rock in Horeb, of the two columns of fire and cloud which rested on the tabernacle. Different meteorological phenomena are supposed to have happened while Mosheh was on a mountain top. Many speeches, laws, regulations, are supposed to have been delivered to the people by a so-called deity.

We will not attempt a description of the historical facts; they are so superbly invented and over-emphasized in the Bible that the whole narrative cannot be taken literally. It is, anyhow, irrelevant. Qabala can see through them.

According to the biblical tale, six hundred thousand armed men, with their wives, their children and their herds, lived forty years in a desert.

When, without any apparent reason, the deity orders a punitive expedition against the Midianites, the booty which is brought back amounts to 675,000 sheep, 720,000 oxen, 61,000 donkeys and 32,000 virgins (mentioned at the end of the enumeration).

So, approximately two million people and an equivalent number of animals are supposed to have spent forty years in a desert, moving their camp more than forty times (Num. xxxiii).

Moreover, the deity requires extraordinary offerings (Exod. xxv) of *gold and silver and brass, and blue, and purple and scarlet, and fine linen, and goat's hair and ram's skins dyed red, and badgers' skins, and shittim wood, oil for the light, spices for anointing oil, and for sweet incense, onyx stones and stones to be set in blue ephod, and in blue breastplate.* . . . And the people must build a sanctuary with a tabernacle, and instruments, and an ark, and staves, and a mercy seat, and cherubims of gold, and a table of shittim wood overlaid with gold, and dishes, and spoons, and a candlestick, and extremely elaborate curtains, and holy garments for Aaron. . . . The description of that which has to be built, wrought, inlaid and set by craftsmen of every kind, requiring every known material of that epoch, is very far indeed from the possibilities open to a huge population living in a desert—and living on manna falling from the skies!

Let us now consider the most human of all the laws which are given to those people (Exod. xx, 13): *Thou shalt not kill*, so many times quoted by so many killers.

It must be observed that the very deity that promulgates that law considers itself as being outside its own jurisdiction. When it intervenes in the history of the Hebrews, it is usually to order wholesale destruction; and Mosheh himself, the giver of the law, negates it whilst giving it.

(Exod. xxxii, 27-28) When Moses sees that because he has "delayed to come down out of the mount", the people and Aaron have fashioned a "molten calf" to worship, he becomes enraged, and he gives this order to the sons of Levi: *Thus says YHWH, the Eloh of Israel, Put every man the sword by his side, and go in and out from gate to gate throughout the camp, and slay every man his brother, and every man his companion, and every man his neighbour.*

On that day about three thousand men were killed.

It is well to remember that at the time the death penalty was inflicted for many breaches of the law which we now consider as being only minor offences. The priests had to slaughter animals every day, and the altar must have been a disgusting sight. The people were driven to a state little short of obsession by innumerable petty regulations to be rigorously observed every day, every hour, in every circumstance of life, and threatening fantastic punishments.

By what strange contrivance of the people, for what unconscious necessity, through what hypnotic influence, is this narrative to be taken at its face value and included in a "Holy" Bible?

The answer is in Exodus xxv, 21-22: *... in the ark*, says YHWH to Mosheh, *thou shalt put the testimony that I shall give thee. And there I will meet with thee, and I will commune with thee. ...*

The Qabala knows that that testimony was itself, the Qabala. Every possible precaution was taken by Mosheh to protect it, physically and morally, with the extreme rigour of intricate laws. He kept the people held in a magical net of authority. No armour could be too strong for the precious Revelation which was deposited in the ark. The way it came to be created can be seen in Exodus xvii, 8-16, where a mysterious Amalek fights with Israel and where Mosheh tells a mysterious Yehoushea (Joshua) to go and fight Amalek.

No explanation is given of who that Amalek might be and no exegesis, except the Qabala, has ever explained YHWH's and Mosheh's very peculiar behaviour in the circumstance: *And YHWH said to Mosheh, write this for a memorial in a book, and rehearse it in the ears of Joshua: for I will utterly put out the remembrance of Amalek from under Shamaim* (heaven). *And Mosheh built an altar, and called the name of it YHWH-nissi: For he said, Because YHWH hath sworn that YHWH will have war with Amalek from generation to generation.*

It is strange indeed to build an altar in remembrance of something that has to be utterly forgotten. And YHWH does not fight Amalek in order to gain victory: he established against him a state of perpetual warfare "from generation to generation". Who, or what, is Amalek?

Then in Exodus xviii, appears Jethro. He comes to Mosheh with his daughter Zifforah and her two sons. *And Mosheh went out to meet his father-in-law and did obeisance.* Later on, Jethro *took*

THE CIPHER OF GENESIS

an offering for Elohim, and *all the elders of Israel* ate bread with
him. Finally, Jethro criticizes Mosheh and instructs him as to
what he has to do. The Yahwic immanence will disappear, and
the evolutionary process of Elohim will be set in motion.

Those episodes, as is always the case when something essential is said in the Bible, are not and cannot be understood by
the synagogues or the churches. They have a threefold meaning
(on three different levels), they describe the transformation of
energy that we have mentioned above in using the term
Sephiroth.

Only a careful study of the letter-numbers used in this narrative can give an adequate understanding of the (enacted)
drama. We shall describe it briefly.

It begins with the fight between the children of Israel and
Amalek: Aam-Lekh, on a certain level, means "that which is
thine". It is an emanation of YHWH. According to YHWH's
custom, it is a test intended to discover the power or resistance
of Mosheh.

Were he, Amalek, an individual, he would be killed and done
for, but YHWH wages an eternal battle against him. Nothing
is so everlasting. YHWH is battling against a "himself" personified by Amalek.

Mosheh, in this contest, needs help. And two "principles"
are within him, personified by Ahron (Aaron) and Hur.
Mosheh fights thus: *When Moses held up his hand, Israel prevailed;
and when he let down his hand, Amalek prevailed* (Exod. xvii, 11-12).
But Mosheh's hands were heavy: and they (Aaron and Hur) *took a
stone and put it under him, and he sat thereon; and Aaron and Hur
stayed up his hands, the one on the one side, and the other on the other
side.*

Thus Joshua vanquished Amalek and his people.

Mosheh then builds an altar to YHWH. We cannot, here,
use any of the translations of this episode. We can only attempt
to give one in accordance with the Qabala. What he says is
approximately this: "YHWH has performed for me a miracle,
but if the hand goes against Yod-Hay, what is the salt of it for

36

me; but with that which is thine, I will be in the existence of two worlds."

These two worlds are Emanation and Creation. It is a certainty, according to the Qabala, that at that moment Mosheh was exactly at the junction of two worlds in apparent opposition. He realized that YHWH was staging a conflict within one single energy. The two worlds in conflict were only one world. So Mosheh could no longer fight, because which ever side he fought against was still YHWH. So he suddenly became quite still.

Now Jethro came to him. The text insists in saying that he is the Cohen of Midian, the Hhoten of Mosheh. Whenever one finds so great an emphasis, its purpose is always to attract our attention. There is something to understand which is beyond the apparent meaning of Jethro being Mosheh's father-in-law. The theme Hhoten expresses, according to its ideograms, is a state of expectancy of the primitive, undifferentiated substance. The transformation of Reuel to Jethro expresses the response of that substance to the action of YHWH upon it. The final Noun in Cohen, Midian, and Hhoten opens the way to possibility. Likewise, Joshua will be called "son of Noun".

It is said, in the translations, that Zifforah, who comes with her father, had been sent back by Mosheh. This is an erroneous interpretation of the text. Even in colloquial Hebrew, the word used is Shiloheya, which here means that Zifforah is liberated. Her second son's name is Elyezer; Elohim helps.

Jethro explains to Mosheh the point of view of the gross human substance which Elohim's process is going to mould so that it can evolve. Mosheh, who only knows YHWH's side of the question, yields entirely to his advice.

We will close this chapter with a reference to Exodus xxiv, 9-11: *Then went up Mosheh, and Ahron, Nadab, and Abihu, and seventy of the elders of Israel.* We see here four principles—or archetypes: (*a*) Mosheh, the cosmic breath saved from the waters; (*b*) Ahron, the pulsation life-death of Aleph, alive in its dwelling and acting in the game in which indetermination is at stake; (c) Nadab, the continuity of existence (and of the Qabala); and (d) Abihu, the living germ of Elohim, within that container.

Those four pseudo-persons *saw the God of Israel: and there was under his feet as it were a paved work of sapphire stone, and as it were the body of heaven in its clearness. And upon the nobles of the children of Israel he laid not his hand: also they saw God, and did eat and drink.*

This is really too crude. A God with feet, therefore a God in a body, is an idol. This passage is an exceedingly ignorant transcription of cabalistic symbols. The "sapphire stone" is the Sepher, the Book. That which is seen and acknowledged is the Qabala.

Mosheh, after this communion, does not climb a physical mountain. He ascends, so to speak in two cosmic lives, in the two lives of Yod-Hay-Vav-Hay.

Mosheh did not cross the Jordan, but the people did, ruled by Joshua, who had become the high priest of their national God.

They invaded the land of Canaan. With that expedition, the real history of the Jews begins, a history of violence, wars, destruction and massacres.

Their God never ceased to tell them, through the mouth of Joshua, that it was *He* who had fought for them, *He* who had exterminated defenceless populations. Had He not stopped the motion of the sun and thrown stones from His heaven so as the better to annihilate the victims of that invasion?

After Joshua's death, YHWH armed the sons of Judah. They attacked Jerusalem, killed its inhabitants, set fire to the town, and began to worship the Baals and the Astartes. YHWH became enraged because of this idolatry. He delivered the sons of Israel into the hands of plunderers and of all their enemies. He deprived them of every means of resistance, he drove them to a state of extreme distress and misery, and he sent Judges to rule over them.

YHWH was with the Judges and protected Israel during their lifetime, because of his compassion for the people. But at the death of each Judge, the sons of Israel became even more corrupt than their fathers had been and incurred the wrath of YHWH.

YHWH, between the extreme Harshness and Clemency, sometimes delivered the people to their enemies, sometimes allowed them to intermingle peacefully with other nations. The result was the same: the sons of Israel always relapsed into idolatry.

The traditional Qabala acknowledges the Judges. Their wisdom was of the Qabala. They were known as *Shofitim*. They acted upon the sons of Israel as a pair of bellows does on a fire which burns but feebly. They projected upon their primitive coarse substance the organic breath of cosmic life. Without this action of the Judges, the Qabala would have been lost.

But everything deteriorates eventually. The last Judges, sons of Samuel, *walked not in his ways, but turned aside after lucre, and took bribes, and perverted judgment* (I. Sam. VIII, 3-7).

Then all the elders . . . came to Samuel . . . and said . . . now make us a king to judge us like all the nations. But the thing displeased Samuel . . . and he prayed . . . and YHWH said: Hearken unto the voice of the people in all that they say unto thee; for they have not rejected thee, but they have rejected me, that I should not reign over them.

In spite of Samuel's strong warnings, the sons of Israel organized themselves into a political state, "like all the nations", and henceforth the name of Israel lost its meaning.

The entire reign of their first king, Saul, was a period of savage, cruel wars. The troubled reign of David ended, however, in a more peaceful period, preparatory to Solomon's ostentatious reign.

Solomon married the daughter of Pharaoh and took her to Jerusalem, where he built his famous temple. He reigned over all Israel, made alliance with the king of Tyre, built cities, accumulated great riches and died after having reigned forty years.

This highest point of kingly glory included seven hundred wives and three hundred concubines, and his reign ended with the division of the country.

Jeroboam, king of Israel, re-established the cult of idols. In this manner he wished to show his independence in the face of Judah. In the meanwhile, Jerusalem passed from a king who "did well" to a king who was *evil in the eyes of YHWH*.

The people alternately worshipped idols and submitted again to the laws of Moses: they refused to "humiliate" themselves before the prophets, then returned to their fear of them.

In the temple, the so-called cult of YHWH consisted of a repetition of formulas. The Qabala lamented, wept and cursed in anger through the prophets, but it remained unknown to the people, the kings, and even to the priests.

There was a coffer at the door of the temple where worshippers used to put coins. One day, under *the money that was brought into the house of YHWH, Hilkiah the priest found a book of the law of YHWH given by Moses* (II Chron. xxxiv, 14).

Ultimately, the movement of the pendulum between YHWH and idols came to a deadlock. It was the end of that "container", of that continuity.

The earthly adventure in Canaan had been (and still is) an error of the people. In those times, it was a necessity for the myth. Had not Jerusalem existed as the holy centre of the Mosaic Law, YHWH would not have destroyed it. Its importance lies in its destruction, not in its having been built.

For Israel in its true sense, the name Canaan is not that of a country. It has no frontiers. And YHWH in its true meaning is not a deity to be worshipped, least of all in a temple.

YHWH, then, realized that Jerusalem as a process could not evolve towards its maturity. Therefore, *he brought upon them the king of the Chaldees* (II Chron. xxxvi, 17), and Nebuchadnezzar slew all people, young or old; and he brought to Babylon all the treasures of the temple and all the treasures of the kings and princes. And the temple was burnt, and all the palaces. Jerusalem was destroyed. The few people who escaped were carried to Babylon, *to fulfil the word of YHWH . . . until the land had enjoyed her sabbaths.*

The land enjoyed 70 years of sabbaths, after which Babylon was defeated by Cyrus. YHWH *stirred up the spirit of Cyrus . . .*

and charged him to build him an house at Jerusalem (Ezra I and II), *and those which had been carried away unto Babylon . . . came again into Jerusalem.*

The fact that Nebuchadnezzar as king of the Chaldees and the symbolic 70 years of captivity are mentioned, show clearly that the sons of Israel who escaped were driven back by the ruler of their pre-natal land. They were, symbolically, thrown back inside the womb, so as to be born again. The 70 years are a sign of renewal. Under that sign, Babylon was destroyed, and Cyrus liberated the captives.

When the sons of Israel returned to Jerusalem, they were "reborn", to an extent that they had forgotten their mother tongue. They did not, however, come to realize what their universal mission was. They began to rebuild the temple, but not without great difficulties and delays.

Eventually, the temple was completed *and all the people gathered themselves together as one man into the street that was before the water gate; and they spake unto Ezra the scribe to bring the book of the law of Moses, which YHWH had commanded to Israel* (Neh. VIII, 1). (Note the symbol "water gate".)

With Ezra, the knowledge of the Qabala re-emerged. It was an understanding of the primordial Revelation, combined with a submission to the laws of Moses. This double connection permitted that very small nation to survive despite the Persian domination.

According to tradition, the Book was rewritten by Ezra, who is said to have given the ideograms the shapes which we know today and to have put together the first five books, partly from oral traditions, partly from written documents.

Then came an historical period similar to many others. Hellenism influenced some of the people. As in every happy period, some Jews became assimilated, others continued to submit to the domination of ritual, and the Qabala once again disappeared from sight.

That period lasted until it was brutally interrupted by the Syrian kings, who embarked upon another period of warfare.

(The memory of Judas Maccabaeus is still alive today.) Jerusalem was captured and freed several times. Revolt succeeded revolt until the conquest of Judah by the Romans.

The history from then on is well known. We come to the destruction of Jerusalem by Titus in A.D. 70, and the ceaseless revolts of the Jews, which culminated, in A.D. 135, with the final destruction of Jerusalem by Hadrian and the Dispersion, or Diaspora.

The first three centuries of our era were a period of intense intellectual activity and of confusion of mind. Judaism was subject to ruptures of all kinds. An Hellenistic-Judaism, opposed to a talmudic rabbinism, both conflicted with a very powerful—although little-known—undercurrent of anti-sacerdotalism, which proclaimed that the universal message of Israel had been betrayed by the party of the Temple.

The author of Barukh's Apocalypse gives orders to all the priests to throw the key of the sanctuary to heaven, and to ask YHWH to preserve the House that they have not been able to hold.

The apocalyptic period did not last. Some took refuge in hope: "the Temple will be rebuilt some day". Craving for its own continuity, the synagogue settled on a few relics of ritualistic prescriptions. The Qabala became secret, occult. That germ of life hid itself in an impenetrable shell.

The outer authority was taken in charge by Instructors: the *Tanaim*. They were the custodians of the Torah, of the Law, of the prescriptions. They did not seek to proselytize. Their field of activity did not extend outside Israel. They had but one aim: the remoulding of an entity, Israel, without a State and without Jerusalem.

Their action was based on the Law and on the Commentaries (which became the part of the Talmud called the *Mishnah*), and on a life of incredible abnegation and sanctity, going as far as martyrdom. (It is enough to remember the names of Rabbi Meir and Akibah.)

It is true that some of those rabbis knew the Qabala in its

42

exoteric sense, based on the laws of Moses better than they knew the original Revelation as it existed in a past more remote than the times of Moses. They believed that the symbolic narrative of Genesis was a description of actual facts, and they read those facts upside down according to their spoken languages; they believed in Adam's sin and the fall of Man, they worshipped a deity which cannot but be anthropomorphized when it is prayed to. The secret code of the Qabala was a closed book for most, except Akibah, and perhaps a few others. But it was necessary that it should be so, that in all their charity, in their intense activity, they might play their part in this drama.

It was because of those meek doctors of the Law that the Gospels were defeated in their attempts to free themselves from the Hebrew myth.

These doctors were so obstinately adamant that the first Christians were compelled to avail themselves of Abraham and to find in him the origin of their creed.

Their wish was the opposite of the syncretism towards which our time seems to direct itself. If they claimed Abraham, it was in the hope of substituting themselves for the people who had made a covenant with YHWH.

The Qabala knows that YHWH is not a deity but an immanence which can become alive and active when the two vitalities in us, the container and the contained, fecundate each other. Historically, those vitalities of Israel came into being when the mistaken expression, material and materializing, of the Temple and of Jerusalem, was destroyed. The Qabala, for the time being, obeyed the Law, and reciprocally the Law held the Qabala in great respect and honour.

Such was the truth of those times: the biological necessity of Israel's mystery. If the first three centuries following the destruction of Jerusalem were the most intense in the life of Israel, it was because everything had been destroyed.

The great initiator of the Qabala in the second century was Simeon-Bar-Yohai. Against the powerful movements called the Talmud and the Qabala, the Christians were helpless.

43

They found all sorts of arguments. They said—erring profoundly—that Abraham's faith was more important than the circumcision, that Abraham is "the father of nations", that the Patriarchs obviously did not obey the Law of Moses, and that, conditioned by these laws, the Jews were only a lateral branch of the human tree.

Interpreting an important theme of Genesis in a certain fashion (which will be explained later on), the Christians proclaimed themselves to be the "eldest" because they had come "after" Israel. Had they been more mature ontologically, they would have had, perhaps, some reason for saying so. But, in fact, they were not mature.

On the Jewish side, other currents were seeking to express themselves. One thought the Law of Moses to be monolithic, and decreed that it must be obeyed in its every detail. They reasoned that, the Temple being destroyed, it was absolutely impossible to follow all the prescriptions, and that therefore it would be a sin to interpret them according to circumstances.

Others said, "Better transform than do nothing; at least, it will help to keep them in memory."

In Alexandria these developed a strong tendency not unlike that of our "reformed" synagogues.

Other Jews declared themselves to be more Jewish than all other Jews, because they were disciples of the Rabbi Jesus, in whom they saw the embodiment of the essence of Israel, which is life-death and resurrection.

We cannot have an adequate idea of the great turmoil which marked the period from approximately the third to the seventh centuries. Its centre was Alexandria. All the documentation of those centuries was stored in its library, which was burned at least three times.

One of the Ptolemys tried to launch a syncretic deity, Serapis, but his attempt did not succeed in reviving the ancient Egyptian religion. Another Ptolemy patronized the translation of the Bible into Greek. According to a legend seventy learned men made seventy absolutely identical translations of it!

Aquila, a disciple of Akibah in the time of Hadrian also made a translation into Greek. A certain Symmacus, at the end of the eighth century, made another translation which was used by a Judaeo-Christian sect.

Thus there were three different versions: the Septuagint, which was the official one in use by the church; Aquila's which was adopted by the Jews of the Diaspora; and that of Symmacus. Later on the Septuagint was accepted by the synagogues of the Diaspora who despised Aquila the proselyte.

Many other Greek versions were made. Origen who spent many years of his life in comparing them and St. Jerome who learned Hebrew for the purpose of a translation into Latin must also be mentioned.

We thus see that the widespread enthusiastic fashion for translations is not a privilege of our own times. As far back as the second century, the synagogues attempted to go towards the outer world rather than to retire into the Talmud. For that purpose, they adopted foreign languages for their liturgy.

Many Jews, however, said that when the version of the Seventy came out it was a time of great sorrow and mourning for the rabbis who knew that the text cannot be translated. They put ashes on their heads, they tore their garments, they wept and cried out that such a sacrilege had never before been committed, not even when the Golden Calf had been set up, that it would have been better not to have been born than to have witnessed the day that the Torah was translated.

Without indulging in such an excessive display of grief, it cannot but be declared that they were perfectly right. The undercurrent of their violent reaction was intensified because the Temple was no more.

The real disciple of Akibah was not Aquila, the proselyte-translator. Akibah is the very source of two parallel trends, thanks to which the Book is still alive. Akibah had two important disciples: Rabbi Meir, the master of the Talmud, and the miraculous Simeon-Bar-Yohai, the "holy lamp of Israel", to whom is attributed the origin of the Zohar, which Moses de

Leon is supposed to have written in Spain in the thirteenth century, according to certain authoritative opinions.

A note of doubt is necessary as far as the origin, dates and authors of cabalistic writings are concerned. For instance, the well known Sepher Yetzirah is known to have been written in a period preceding the birth of Islam, at any time between the sixth century B.C. and the sixth century of our era. Any scientific research within so wide a margin is hopeless.

The Sepher Yetzirah is a very short text which emerges from the thick forest of the Talmud and the Zohar. It is mentioned because it is characteristic of the way in which cabalists deliberately enrobed their knowledge in cryptic and apparently absurd utterances.

An attempted English translation of its first lines would read approximately thus: "By thirty-two mysterious paths of wisdom, Yah, the Lord of Armies, God alive . . . has engraved and created His world with three Sepharim . . . ten Sephiroth Belimah and twenty-letters of foundation", etc. . . .

We have repeatedly stated that the letters of the Hebrew alphabet have always been, throughout the centuries, the foundation of the true tradition and the only key to the knowledge of the Hebrew Revelation.

Of course, the statement that a deity created the Universe by means of the Hebrew alphabet is literally absurd. It can be expressed differently in stating that every letter is, in fact, an ideogram which symbolizes one aspect of the cosmic energy. Thus we know where to look for meaning and purpose of the biblical text: it describes the interplay of those energies in the Universe and in Man. Thus we free our minds from all mystical imaginings. In following the text we then are subjected to an amazing mental exercise which can modify our way of thinking to the extent of uniting us with those very energies which are being described. That, and that only, is the Revelation.

At all times the rabbinical principle has held that nothing in the Genesis is there by mere chance or by mistake; nothing is useless; every repetition has its purpose; and the different grammatical mistakes according to the Hebrew language are no mistakes at all: when read according to code they reveal their meaning.

Every epoch has its own way of understanding things and of feeling them. When truth is met it is expressed differently according to the stage of mental and emotional developments of the period. In ancient times symbols, parables, metaphors, images, legends may have conveyed a meaning for the understanding. We, today, need a psychological and rational approach. Therefore it is useless—and, we venture to say, harmful—for us to dally with interpretations of interpretations of what people have supposed to be revelations put forward by Abraham, Moses or Jesus.

We have not the time to spend in the consideration of antiquated approximations to knowledge. Therefore no mere student of Qabala will ever understand the Qabala from within. Were he to read and re-read the Zohar, learn all about Simeon-Bar-Yohai, Moses of Leon, Abraham, Abulafia or Knorr von Rosenroth's *Kabbala Denudata*, he would be trying to see by looking through the wrong end of a telescope.

Nothing is important except the knowledge that the key to that Revelation is to be found in the letter-numbers. When once we grasp that, we can grope our way through them, and our very first step will already have been taken inside their cosmic life.

That Revelation is timeless and is therefore of all time. One cannot contact it if it is imagined to have happened in the past. It is of now when we accept it to be of now. Unless we are fully of our time we are seeking it in its tracks on the sands of time.

The situation of the twentieth-century man in relation to the Bible is entirely different from what it was in the second century. In those times the early Christians were trying to dissociate themselves from the Jews who had been deprived of their Church. They proclaimed that the destruction of the Temple had been a punishment and that a new Church must take the place of the old.

We have already seen some of their arguments. Their opposition to the Jews developed and intensified to the point of degenerating into a theological anti-semitism. The Jews became hated because they "had murdered God". With John Chrysostom, the Christian exegesis at its lowest level became a purely abusive oratory. According to YHWH's well-known reactions it stirred the rabbis to a still greater energy. They taught:

"Do the Christians appeal to Abraham? The Qabala dedeclares itself prior to him."

"Is Mosaic law only a lateral branch of the human tree? On the contrary, it is the protective shell of the living Revelation."

"Does faith save? Not at all. Only the Covenant with YHWH is life."

"Are the ritual prescriptions a punishment? Of course not: they prove YHWH's love for his people."

"Is Christianity the true Israel, as it attempts to say? But when, how, in what circumstance has it wrestled with Elohim and defeated him, as Jacob did when he deserved and received that name: Israel?"

From the second century until the Middle Ages the Qabala spread in every direction. Eastward, it went to Egypt, Asia Minor, Arabia, Persia and as far as India. It can be found in the Quran, and it is established that the Prophet Mohammad had been taught by Rabbis. It was carried by the Jews and Arabs into Spain, to the south of France and as far as the Anglo-Saxon world.

The end of the fourteenth century was the beginning of tragic times for the Jews. They were persecuted in Spain and expelled. They sought refuge wherever they could find it.

It was again for the Qabala a period of confusion and decline all over Europe. Although it was respected by some free minds among philosophers, alchemists and a few mystics, it degenerated into a symbolic caricature of occultism and, with the added attacks of the anti-semites, it died an ignoble death in cheap modern novels.

It had not died everywhere. By a strange historical freak, it reappeared in Egypt when Isaac Loria discovered the Zohar in Cairo. The school of Safed, which he founded, re-established the broken link between the observance of rites and the Shekinah (YHWH's exile from this earth). The school eventually degenerated into an excessive asceticism, alien to the true knowledge of the Qabala.

The state of symbiosis between Knowledge and Law had come to an end.

The last blow was given by the Jewish scholars of the nineteenth century belonging to the rational school of Judaeo-German origin. This school of thought is still in existence today, and is backed by Zionism, by the synagogues and by the official voice of International Judaism.

It considers that the cabalistical tradition in its totality is a mystical rambling which has been a poison for Israel.

This rationalism is partly responsible for the picture, common to some religions, of a YHWH reduced to an avatar of Zeus or Jupiter, sitting in a heaven. But YHWH in the true sense of its letter-code schema, cannot be corrupted by any wrong usage which is made of it. Rationalization is a corruption in itself.

The knowledge that is called Qabala must no longer be reduced to a mere subject of study for seekers of recondite mysteries. It must now come to full light and penetrate serious minds.

The synagogues can only ignore it because they have repudiated intelligence. They keep on reading and commenting on an archaic law which has no reality. The real knowledge of the Qabala recedes further and further every day because of the foolish teachings of amateur scholars who, having learned a few tricks which can be played with the letter-numbers, amuse the public with their speculations, or entertain their readers with strange stories concerning some ancient Rabbi.

The modern Rabbis have become archivists of formulas and preachers of conventional morality. We believe that most of them are quite ignorant of esoteric rabbinism, and of its many

49

interpretations, quite aside from the plain reading of the Book.

A Christian Qabala has been attempted in vain, its roots being artificial. It was intended as a substitute for the Hebrew rather than as an authentic penetration into the Scriptures.

As to the new settling of a State in the geographical Canaan, it can be understood because of the abominable slaughter ordered under the Nazi regime. From a human point of view, it corresponds to a necessity for survival and to the recurring wish expressed unto Samuel to be like unto the other nations.

It is to be hoped that to these "husbandmen" of the earth, YHWH will say what he said to Jonah: *And should I not spare Nineveh, that great city, wherein are more than six score thousand persons that cannot discern between their right hand and their left hand, and also much cattle?*

*

In brief, the Qabala today can be reborn neither in the Synagogue nor in the State that calls itself Israel. Both ignore it, so it ignores them. It has no valid motive for conforming to the very few Mosaic prescriptions which still survive and which every conforming Jew interprets according to his fancy.

It must offer itself freely to minds which are free. It is no longer mysterious and occult. On the contrary, it is intelligible and marvellously intelligent. It is the very source of the civilizations that have gravitated around the Mediterranean which are today spreading all over our planet.

It states the religious problem as it has to be stated in a time when the further the horizon recedes, the nearer we come to the Mystery.

For such minds as are no longer bounded by ancient horizons and have thus become a mystery unto themselves, the totality of life is present in action. It is the Soliloquy of the One.

This is the true Revelation, plainly visible to all.

PART TWO

THE BOOK OF GENESIS

I

The Letter-Code

THIS WORK offers a fundamental re-reading of the text of the Bible's Book of Genesis and some of its consequences in understanding the Gospels of Matthew and John. The revolutionary meanings here presented will be of great significance, it is hoped, to those of the Christian, Hebrew and Moslem religions whose thinking has been conditioned by and rooted in the Bible. And they will be of equal importance to those non-orthodox believers and non-believers whose intelligence has so baulked at the traditionally accepted but unsatisfactory versions of the cosmic drama, to the extent that they have felt it necessary to repudiate the whole of Genesis which they are inclined to consider as being only ancient legends.

Perhaps humanity, for all these centuries, has not been ready to receive the stupendous implications arising from the true content of this book. The first point to be made is that, differing in this respect from many other so-called sacred works which, whether or not rightly understood, can at least be read in their original language, the first five chapters of Genesis have been, more than many others, open to incorrect interpretation because they are not written in words which can be translated into any ordinary language.

It may come as a surprise to many Bible readers that these five chapters were written in code and cannot be deciphered without knowledge of the code. Each letter of the Hebrew alphabet represents a specific number, the significance of which must be understood—a not too difficult process, as will be seen later on. These numbers are not to be considered in their arithmetical sense. Each one, in fact, signifies an aspect of living forces at play in the Universe; and the text is intended to project these forces into our very being, thus acting as a Revelation. This process, being based in Reality, does not involve the projection of an idea. It has nothing to do with a creed; for the only principles by which it is bound are universal.

The original text deals with states of consciousness and their relationship to life as it happens now. It does not deal with anything that happened in the past. Life is *now*, and if there is anything that can be called Revelation, it cannot be an illusory explanation of what has already happened, but it is an incursion of the life process into our actual being.

The very existence of the Universe is a gigantic fact and mystery that can never be fathomed by human thought. That fact must be faced squarely, and not explained away, because so-called explanations pile mystery upon mystery and delude the mind, creating the habit of *thinking* about that which it cannot ever *conceive*.

Seen in its true light, the first verse of the Bible has an entirely different significance from that conveyed by the inadequate translation familiar to us from childhood: *In the beginning, God created the heaven and the earth*. This translation does not make sense at all, because it is unthinkable. A "beginning" of time and space is as unthinkable as is their non-beginning. Therefore, a text which proclaims the hopelessly inconceivable leads at the very start into the fictitious domains of wrong thinking. Even the word "God" is inconceivable, obviously so. The hypothesis of the existence of an unthinkable God previous to an unthinkable beginning forces the mind to confront the absurdity of a something-before-anything creating everything out of nothing.

Thus—by means of such circuitous strategems—does the psyche mesmerize the intellect so as to extort the justifications it requires in order to avoid having to face the dreaded idea of an ever-present mystery. It uses the same devious ways when shaping into symbols and images the abstract notions expressed by the original ideograms. The psyche's structure being fundamentally sensorial, its utterances in any language cannot but exteriorize its irrational longings and fears. (This fact appears when one considers that many roots of the Hebrew language have two contradictory meanings and that dynamic schemata mean for the psyche an overturning of protective structures.)

The cosmic and human drama as described in the Bible is an interplay between two partners playing against each other: *Aleph*, intermittent life-death, unfathomable, timeless mystery evading all mental grasp, and *Yod*, its projection into the time-space continuum, which is its antinomy. The winner, obviously, is always *Aleph* because all that exists must of necessity come to an end. But the psyche, dreaming of an indefinite duration—in the form of an eternal soul, for example—rejects the very notion of its own death and clings to philosophies or religions that encourage it to believe that the word "always" has a meaning.

The traditional reading of the Bible is the result of intellectual subjugation to psychological demands. The Book of Genesis when read according to custom therefore appears in the form of a story relating the facts and gestures of such people as Adam, Eve, Cain, Abel, and so forth, but whose names when read in the light of the cabalistic code reveal that they are abstract formulas of cosmic energy focused in the human psyche.

An example can illustrate this point; in the first chapter of Genesis it is repeatedly written: "and God said". There is no such word as God in the book. The schema *Elohim*, (*Aleph-Lammed-Hay-Yod-Mem*), as will be exhaustively shown later, is the process through which *Aleph* becomes *Yod* in evolutionary existence, and the schema *Yomer* (*Yod-Aleph-Mem-Raysh*) which is translated "said" is an emanation of both *Yod* and *Aleph* in a state of existence and life.

(The schema *Yod-Hay-Vav-Hay* translated "the Lord" or Jehovah, which appears in Genesis II, expresses an existence fulfilled by two lives [Hay and Hay] of psyche and body mutually fecundating one another. When this happens YHWH is alive in us.)

55

When decoded the letter-numbers are of such a nature as to be able to satisfy our intellect but their import can only reveal itself in the depths of our beings. They first appear in Genesis as archetypes pre-existent to any articulate language, but these gradually condense (or reduce) into allegories which in turn become constituent parts of an epic poem in which Abraham, Isaac, Jacob and their wives are the principal protagonists. This metaphysical narrative has come to be considered as being a series of episodes in the chronicles of an ancient Semitic tribe and continue to be looked upon for no apparent reason as being an important chapter in holy Scriptures of world-wide traditional beliefs.

Much later Rabbi Jesus hoped to promote a revival based on the original revelation of light in Man, which met with massive resistance originating not only in Hellenistic paganism but also on the part of the Hebrews who had forgotten the essentials of their own religion. John's gospel treats the subject of human consciousness as related to the myth of inner light.

Following these preliminaries we can now further investigate the purpose of this essay.

2

The Challenge

HEBREW writing has no numerals to indicate numbers. These are expressed by the letters of the Hebrew alphabet, each letter corresponding to a number. The origin of these numbers, so we believe, goes back to an epoch long prior to history, and ancient tradition purports to show their significance, which is that each number has a meaning in relation to cosmic forces. A similar tradition is found at the origin of the civilization of ancient Egypt. None can say whence it arose. Gradually it was lost in the course of the centuries, and the deep significance that each number was intended to convey has disappeared. Only the significance of each letter, itself composed of several alphabetical characters, has remained but in a state of degraded meaning. As an example, we have Bayt = House; but the numbers are not understood beyond their numerical meaning. The principal reason for this is that the correct reading of these numbers as they occur in word sequence is difficult, to say the least. It inflicts an unwanted exercise upon the mind crystallized by habit and inertia.

Our ordinary thinking process is concerned with descriptions of things and not with the things themselves. If we are speaking of movement we do not transmit a movement, but only the idea of movement. If we speak of music, of colour, of all that one can feel or see, we evoke in another person the images, the feelings, the symbols which have attached themselves to something similar which they remember or already know (thus producing comparison). If we say, for instance, (Gen. 1, 2) that *Darkness was upon the face of the deep*, we evoke a familiar image of night and a thought of obscure spaces. Thus what is given us is not darkness itself nor do we create a great abyss; we only call upon imagination, and each person proceeds to imagine what he wishes to imagine or what he is capable of imagining!

When communication purports to convey *the* Revelation such ambiguity can only lead to one or another of the multifarious religious interpretations which obstruct the immediate perception of the fact that the very existence of a speck of dust is in very truth the first and the last mystery. No mystery is greater than any other: the Qabala has always known it, and has therefore never raised the question as to whether God exists. For those of the Qabala, for Abraham, Moses or Jesus, the unknowable unknown is a presence. The knowing of that presence is the unknown. There is no other revelation. It is therefore and above all necessary to reject all interpretations, explanations, creeds and dogmas, all faiths and moral laws, all traditions, philosophies and theologies, so as to allow the unknown to operate directly in our minds. Then thought is free to observe the interplay of life and death and existence because it moves along with it, having shattered its fetters. The Qabala postulates that knowledge is not a formulation but a cosmic energy imparted to the mind by the letter-numbers.

Thus it is useless for the mind to try to formulate ideas about transcendence, which is totally beyond comprehension or measure. Whatever ideas of it one may think one has attained one can have only a notion of greater, better, etc. In the first place, any notion of perfection and timelessness we may form is bound to be invalidated by our inveterately dualistic mode of thought. Our whole idea of progress is based on the idea that the good is simply that which awaits us at the opposite end of a continuum which starts with the not-good. Imperfection and time do not merely enter our thoughts; they *are* our thoughts. Like any other mere tool, the mind as we use it is functionally identical with its products. The chicken and the egg of the mind produce and reproduce one another *ad infinitum, ad nauseam.*

As long as we are not in direct contact with that which transcends the human mind, the fundamental significance of life escapes us. But that primordiality invades us as soon as we decipher the first letter of the first schema of the Revelation, and the witnessing of it is the part of having it revealed, because, after all, the revelation is always there but for its being witnessed.

There is no transcendence other than our intimacy with the unknown as the unknown. Seeking it is avoiding it. It is ever-lastingly present in an ever present genesis. Let us therefore re-read that Book, not as an archaic attempt to describe an un-witnessed creation of the world by a soliloquizing deity but as a penetration of vital energies at work in ourselves.

★

In the present book, we wish to show that the original tradi-tion of the Book of Genesis was a correct presentation of a cer-tain trend of thought; that this tradition was subsequently lost; that the Rabbi Yhshwh better known as Jesus, knew it; that he tried in vain to expound his truth (was it not written that his disciples understood him not?); that his teaching was sub-merged by paganism; that the Christian religion is but a modi-fied form of paganism; that the Jewish religion has degenerated into a practice of prescribed ritual; that Islam, which claims to be a revival of Abraham's revelation, is rather a social and political phenomenon; and that the cabalists and the Jewish mystics have searched for and, each in his own way, have found the true primordial plan. Finally we believe that the exact meaning of the original tradition can be made apparent today. This discovery may indeed be occurring at the right time. We are at a turning-point of history. We are faced with a change of cycle calling for a renewal of man, requiring that he be bathed in the Source. Thus a many-dimensional challenge con-fronts us. What is first of all demanded of us is—rather than a search for absolute truth—a rooting-out of past errors, a re-linquishing of long-cherished illusions.

To think erroneously regarding a subject of vital importance is to think erroneously in all domains of existence. The prime objective of this Qabala is to show that all the versions of the Bible (particularly of Genesis), including the Hebrew, are in error, and that the original text is marvellously intelligible and intelligent. It has been the source of many civilizations preceding ours and it is the source out of which the future must inevitably be born.

We hope that the meaning of the biblical text will become apparent from chapter five onwards. We shall have to proceed step by step because the key of its Revelation is not to be snatched from a code but can only operate when constantly recreated by its very usage. The unceasing reading through centuries of disordered translations has made it difficult indeed to effect a new beginning in the texture of thought where religion is concerned.

After having somewhat transcribed Genesis we will in a later part of the book attempt an approach to Gnosticism and to one or two sections of the Gospels of Matthew and John, the evidences of which will, we hope, be a contribution to the understanding of essentials.

3

The Letter-Numbers

THE PRESENT writer, being obliged to use our language in order to make himself understood, cannot offer the reader the truth of Genesis, but only images of that truth. Our language is of sensuous origin. By its use, we can only understand by means of imagery. Nevertheless we shall do our best not to stray into illusory beliefs and dreams of the supernatural.

Let us now concern ourselves with the individual Hebrew letter-numbers according to the code.*

The first nine letters are the archetypes of numbers from 1 to 9.

Aleph, no. 1, is the unthinkable life-death, abstract principle of all that is and all that is not.

Bayt† (or Vayt), no. 2, is the archetype of all "dwellings", of all containers: the physical support without which nothing is.

Ghimel, no. 3, is the organic movement of every Bayt animated by Aleph.

Dallet, no. 4, is physical existence, as response to life, of all that, in nature, is organically active with Ghimel. Where the structure is inorganic Dallet is its own resistance to destruction.

Hay, no. 5, is the archetype of universal life. When it is conferred upon Dallet, it allows it to play the game of existence, in partnership with the intermittent life-death process.

Vav (or Waw), no. 6, expresses the fertilizing agent, that which impregnates. It is the direct result of Hay upon Dallet.

Zayn, no. 7, is the achievement of every vital impregnation: this number opens the field of every possible possibility.

* See chart, p. 62.
† We consider this spelling more phonetically correct than the usually adopted Beth.

THE LETTER-NUMBERS

Letter	Value	Letter	Value	Letter	Value
Aleph	1	Yod	10	Qof	100
Bayt Vayt	2	Kaf Khaf	20	Raysh	200
Ghimel	3	Lammed	30	Seen Sheen	300
Dallet	4	Mem	40	Tav	400
Hay	5	Noun	50	final Khaf	500
Vav or Waw	6	Sammekh	60	final Mem	600
Zayn	7	Ayn	70	final Noun	700
Hhayt	8	Pay Phay	80	final Phay	800
Tayt	9	Tsadde	90	final Tsadde	900

Hhayt, no. 8 is the sphere of storage of all undifferentiated energy, or unstructured substance. It expresses the most un-evolved state of energy, as opposed to its achieved freedom in Zayn.

Tayt, no. 9, as archetype of the primeval female energy, draws its life from Hhayt and builds it gradually into struc-tures.

Such is the fundamental equation set and developed in Genesis.

The following nine letters, from Yod no. 10, to Tsadde no. 90, describe the process of the nine archetypes in their factual, conditioned existence: their projections in manifestation are always multiples of 10.

The nine multiples of 100 express the exalted archetypes in their cosmic states.

The number 1000, is written with an enlarged Aleph (Aleph, in Hebrew, actually means a thousand), but is seldom used. It expresses a supreme power, a tremendous cosmic energy, all-pervading, timeless, unthinkable.

The study of those multiples by 10 and by 100 is therefore the study of the very archetypes in their various spheres of emanation. The student will find it useful to examine them, so to say, vertically: 1.10.100-2.20.200 . . . and so on.

The choice of Kaf (20) for 500, of Mem (40) for 600, and of Noun (50) for 700 in finals of schemata means that those numbers acquire such cosmic values when they unfold in human beings. Thus: Adam is 1.4.40 when immature and achieves 1.4.600 when attaining his full maturity.

Here is a brief general view of the relationship between the archetypes and their multiples:

Aleph-Yod-Qof (1.10.100): Whereas Aleph (1) is the beat, or pulsation life-death-life-death, Yod (10) is its projection in temporal continuity. So Yod (in Hebrew: the hand), is the opposite of Aleph, its partner playing against it the game with-out which nothing would be. The Qof (100) is the most difficult symbol to understand. It includes Aleph exalted in its principle yet acting through its projection, against itself, and thereby being cosmically deathless. It is best seen in Qaheen (Cain) that mythical destroyer of illusions.

Bayt-Kaf-Raysh (2.20.200): Whereas Bayt (2), the archetype of all containers, has its roots in the cosmic resistance to life, Kaf (20)—in Hebrew, the hollow of the hand—is ready to receive all that comes and Raysh (200), the cosmic container of all existence, has its roots in the intense organic movement of the universe.

Ghimel-Lammed-Sheen (3.30.300): these three letter-numbers express a movement in progressive enlargement, from the uncontrolled functional action of Ghimel (3), through the controlled connecting agent Lammed (30), going as far as the universal Sheen (300), mythically considered to be the "spirit", or "breath" of God.

Dallet-Mem-Tav (4.40.400): the physical resistance of structures, Dallet (4) finds its purveyor in the maternal waters, Mem (40), where all life originates. Tav (400) is the exaltation of the entire cosmic existence in its utmost capacity to resist to life-death. The root Dallet-Mem (Dam) is "blood" in Hebrew and the root Mem-Tav (Met) is "death". Thus the two together express the complete cycle of existence.

Hay-Noun-Kaf in finals (5.50.500): the universal life, Hay (5) is condensed in individual existences as Noun (50) and is exalted cosmically as Kaf (500) in terminals.

Waw-Sammekh-Mem in finals (6.60.600): Waw (6) is the male agent of fertility, Sammekh (60) the female. Mem when in terminals (600) is the cosmic achievement of fruitfulness both in the intelligent or immaterial part of man and in the flesh. In Hebrew, Waw maintains its character grammatically as copulative or connecting agent.

Zayn-Ayn-Noun in finals (7.70.700): Zayn (7) as an opening towards all possible possibilities has its source and its vision in Ayn (70), which is the word for "eye" in Hebrew. It is exalted in Noun (700); this number expresses the very principle contended for in the interplay of energies throughout the universe:

the principle of indetermination in which life itself is at stake. Here we find Cain again.

Hhayt-Pay-Phay in finals (8.80.800): in every sphere of the emanation, from the densest to the most rarefied essence, these numbers stand for the primordial substance, the unfathomed reserve of undifferentiated, unstructured energy.

Tayt-Tsadde-Tsadde in finals (9.90.900): these ideograms express a progression ascending from the simplest and most primitive cell (or female structural energy) up to the trans-figured symbols of womanhood, social and mythical.

The Book of Genesis begins with a series of letter-numbers that form a schema that is read *Bereshyt* and does not mean "in the beginning". It comprises Bayt (2), Raysh (200), Aleph (1), Sheen (300), Yod (10), Tav (400). Let us look at each one separately.

Bayt (2): Everything that exists is the conditioning of life and the life of the conditioning. Everything that is exists both in-ternally and externally. Each germ of life has an envelope, which derives its movement from the great cosmic force of resistance to the life which is surging up from within (If the shell does not offer the right measure of resistance, the chicken will not hatch.) This whole duality of existence—and of our own thought—is conveyed by no. 2.

Raysh (200): As 2 multiplied by a hundred, *Raysh* represents the totality of the Universe, of interstellar space, of the myriads of stars and all the planets; all is conditioning of life and the life of conditioning. This is a great cosmic dwelling of life, which retains life manifested in accordance with its capacity (200). It includes the totality of nature, all existence: the myriads and myriads of water-drops, of blades of grass, of living cells, and the infinite myriads of elements living in the living elements of algae. *Raysh* (spelt *Raysh-Yod-Sheen*) gives birth to *Sheen*, the great cosmic breath that is everywhere and in everything.

Aleph (1): And behold: In this immense Dwelling, within these innumerable dwellings, everywhere there is creative immanence, spontaneous, always fresh and new; imperishable

65

pulsation of life; recurrent sparks; life-death, life-death, death and resurrection: elusive, timeless. Its manifestation can be perceived and thought of only in this manner.

The non-thinkable has for its symbol the *Aleph* (1). The *Aleph* is always itself and never itself. It is ever recurring, though never the same. *Aleph* creates, it is creation, it is not created, yet it exists. It has no existence because all existence is continuous. It has no memory, having no past. It has no purpose, having no future. If one retains it, it remains retained. If one buries it, it remains buried. If one sets aside its obstacles, it is action. It breaks down resistances, though resistances are never broken by it. Without these, *Aleph* does not become manifest. Without *Aleph*, there would be nothing at all. Such is the image of the *Aleph*. *Aleph* itself is beyond all consciousness, human or cosmic. The image of *Aleph* is only an image, for *Aleph* belongs neither to time nor to space. *Aleph* is beyond the realm of our thought, beyond the reach of our mind.

Sheen (300): Prodigious cosmic motion. Movement of everything that exists. All organisms live through *Sheen* (300), either through or against its action, because *Sheen* is similar to a powerful breath which vivifies and carries away. Only the most extreme weakness can elude or oppose it.

Yod (10): Existence which both betrays and satisfies life. Continuity in the duration of that which duration destroys. *Yod*, projection of *Aleph*, confers reality upon all that tends to bury *Aleph* (dead or alive). Temporal *Yod* (10) is the finite which never rejoins the infinite. *Yod* is the manifested existence in time of *Aleph*, the timeless, the immeasurable.

Tav (400): *Tav* is the cosmic resistance to the life-breath which animates it. Without this resistance of *Tav* (400), life could not come into existence. This resistance to life is that which enables life to produce its prodigiously varied manifest forms.

Such is a first glimpse of the untranslatable *Bereshyt*.

*

Since the profound meaning of each letter must be grasped fully and individually before considering it in its syntax, we now suggest the following reflections concerning the very first letter of the Book of Genesis, *Bayt* (2). If we fully understand this letter-number we will not let our mind indulge in irrelevant speculation, but will resolutely face the problem of finding out whether the human mind has or has not a significance in the universe.

Both the writer and the reader of this book are, no doubt, seated somewhere and aware of their surroundings; this is the exterior aspect of no. 2. Our thought is functioning within our psyche, and also within our body—again no. 2. The psyche, crystallized as it is in self-perception, says "I am I". Our brain, encased in its skull, observes our seated body engaged in reading or writing and says, "This is I". Our own thought is the container of our consciousness. We are entities made up of many dwellings and in spite of the life which is in us we identify ourselves with those dwellings. But can we investigate them in order to uncover our life within? This is the inner search within *Bayt* (2).

But "beyond us" we are aware of a whole Universe, *Raysh* (200), cosmic container of a life that eludes all explanation. It is a fact that we cannot understand how it is that anything at all exists. After having eliminated all the secondary problems, however important—such as our sustenance—we turn to this fundamental problem of life comprehension. It is then that we discover that the only instrument at our disposal for tackling this problem is ourselves.

In order to show us what this instrument is made of, Genesis proposes a total reversal of our so-called thinking, which for thousands of years has immersed us in our dreams. This reversal may be understood by asking ourselves whether all the phenomena of our consciousness—our ideas, beliefs and opinions, our reasonings and points of view, our dislikes and preferences (belonging to a club, to a church, to a business, to the colour of a skin, to a society and a nation, etc.)—whether all these are elements contained in our mind, or if, on the contrary, they are our "containers". If all these are our containers, what about us? Where are we left? Our beings are just résumés, resultants of these dwellings.

Such are some of the quests which arise from *Bayt*, the beginning graph in Genesis, and we must here venture to lay emphasis on this first ideogram because in it is already contained the whole Revelation, if we realize that we actually are that *Bayt* and if we feel the urge to go into it in us.

The initial *Bayt* will ever be a barrier if not an opening, a protective rock if not the solvent of the definitions of ourselves which petrify the roots of our being thrust into them.

One must die while passing the threshold of *Bayt*, or, at the very least, for the reading of the Qabala to have any sense at all, one must feel in oneself the wish to go futher and more deeply into the investigation of what *Bayt* is to us, because *Bayt* is the physical support of *Aleph* without which *Aleph* has no existence.

When we understand the dwelling, the *Bayt*, we see that thinking belongs to the field of what can be seen, felt, measured. Then thought becomes very keen, very active, because it exercises itself in its proper function instead of losing all reason in trying to scale the skies: it does not go chasing after Truth with a capital T; for ordinary common sense knows that truth is re-established when one has uncovered error.

In the matter of these dwellings, our bodies, we can only learn to keep them in good condition by not identifying ourselves with bad habits. If the "I" cannot do without tobacco or drink or without artificially exciting the sexual urge, it identifies itself with sensations and pursuits which it exploits for its own psychological purposes: pleasures, ambitions, social reform, etc. The "I" forgets, or rather does not wish to know, that it *is* this sick body. The resultant illness or state of self-deception is commonly called a neurosis.

The fact of knowing that we are this *Bayt*, this container of life, this body, liberates the body and liberates us from our own selves. A fundamental truth recurrent throughout the Book of

Genesis is that life, inside as well as outside of this container, is unknowable and immeasurable. If we know its implications, we know ourselves: *Bayt* is what we are. We therefore do not possess any of the redeeming "spiritual" attributes invented by the escapist mind. Yet by knowing that which we are, we can allow that which we are not—but which is *in* us—to reveal itself through us.

There are no obscure dragons inside of us with which we must do battle; neither is there any evil that we must obliterate. Nor are the latest techniques for self-improvement or self-fulfilment, the way to liberation. All such struggle and striving, however lofty the conscious motivation, is aimed at establishing a continuity of existence and is consequently in perfidious opposition to the discontinuous life in us, which can only *be* in the newness and freshness of deaths and resurrections. This life, in the Book of Genesis, is named *Aleph*.

The code letters are not limited to a phonetic function in series which have the appearance of words or phrases, although they can be (and are) thus misread. In the instance we are considering at present, the succession *Bayt Raysh Aleph Sheen Yod Tav*—which is constantly read *Bereshyt* and translated "in the beginning"—each letter-number is the name of a cosmic energy acting both outside of us and within us, and each one of these cosmic energies is very complex. Thus the name *Bayt* includes *Yod*, *Tav* as its components. The name *Yod* includes *Waw*, *Dallet*.* In *Dallet* is *Lammed*, *Tav*. In *Lammed* is *Mem*, *Dallet* . . . etc. All such analysis breaks down into letters, the components of which are repetitive (as *Mem*, *Noun*, *Vav*, *Tav*) or simple (as *Hay*). The combination of these residual terms reveals the meaning of the foundations, as it were, of the letters which are being analysed, or, to put it differently, the essence of the cosmic energy which they express.

Thus the language of this text is as complex as life itself, and yet the vital experience which can result from the full percep-

* *Waw* is the same letter of the Hebrew alphabet as *Vav*. They are used interchangeably, since the sound is somewhere between V and W.

tion of it has the simplicity and immediacy of a revelation. The difficulty for the writer will be to elucidate for his readers a text in a language which they do not know, and the difficulty for his readers will be to be compelled to enter into this language before having learned it. In fact, it is a language to be entered into and not to be learned. Its impact is direct, instantaneous and total if we meet it with a mind completely void and are willing to listen to a story which was originally intended to convey something altogether different from what we are conditioned to believe.

In the original meaning, there is no reference to a personal God; woman does not issue from a rib of Adam; she is not called Eve in the Garden of Eden; she does not disobey; there is no question of sin; the woman is not expelled from Eden; Cain does not kill Abel; he is not cursed by a divinity, but on the contrary protected; and if we jump a few hundred centuries to enter the allegory of Yhshwh, better known as Jesus, we find that the only Apostle who aided him in the fulfilment of his enterprise was called Judas. Such statements are no doubt surprising, but it is not generally realized to what extent the notions that Eve disobeyed, that Cain killed Abel and that Judas was a traitor have poisoned the mind. In a fundamental respect, these distortions are still contributing to the emotional illness and psychological disorders of the present-day world.

This and many other such misunderstandings have been brought about by an erroneous way of thinking which, since the dawn of history, it has been the general custom of mankind to follow. This way of thinking involves a usage of words whose meaning it is not possible to conceive. It gave birth to all of the early deities, as well as the latest and the most elaborate theologies. Whereas rational thought cannot but be confined within the field of time and measurement, comparison and evaluation, this erroneous thinking (as already pointed out) makes use of such exalted words as immortality, eternity, absolute, God—and innumerable other vague and emotional projections.

The language we need to use in re-reading the Book of Genesis should preclude all such errors. We shall be careful never to use a word unless its full meaning is clearly grasped. We shall hold to plain common sense and factual statements in order to keep our balance during an exploration which will cut across many deep-rooted fixations in "the thoughts of man".

4

The Thoughts of Man

I⊤ ɪs the purpose of all ciphers to invest a few signs with much meaning. A peculiarity of the Book of Genesis is that it begins with a very strict and close code and gradually develops and unfolds its fifty chapters through symbols and allegories and finally through semi-historical tales.

In the severity of its beginning, in its first chapter, in its first verse, in its first sequence of letter-numbers, is the seed, and in the seed is the whole. This whole can be (and is expected to be) grasped in the *Bayt Raysh Aleph Sheen Yod Tav* of *Bereshyt*. This sequence is in the Revelation and *is* the Revelation, and those who grasp it are in the Revelation and are, in action the Revelation itself.

It is in effect a formula, or rather a fundamental equation of the interplay between *Aleph* and *Yod*. *Aleph*, timeless pulsation life-death-life-death, is shown in the first three graphs *Bayt-Raysh-Aleph* in its surging motion of creative energy, and *Yod*, the evolutionary process of existence is held, so to speak, between the hammer of cosmic metabolism, *Sheen*, and the anvil of its resistant container, *Tav*.

The complete schema goes beyond a mere formula affirming the equivalence of those two terms; its sweeps beyond every duality by amalgamating *Aleph* and *Yod* and making them one. The very formulation of that equation is therefore its solution. In spite of being introduced by means of an intellectual approach it can project in us the essential game of life and existence if we will allow it to break up our every-day linear way of thinking.

The six graphs of *Bereshyt* do not express different ideas

linked one to another by a logical sequence. They do not belong to any time process. They are simultaneous and can therefore be permuted so as to form different schemata, each one of them significant. But these developments cannot be considered here. It will be enough to examine the equation *Bereshyt* just as it is written.

There is no delusion in it because the Revelation is not a fantastic message from a supernatural world. Surely the fantastic thing is to be alive and yet not to know what life is. The whole mystery of life is within us, and yet we search for revelations concerning it in books. Does thinking or speaking about God give us any knowledge of what God is? Are we surprised to discover that the human mind is in a state of total contradiction? We are living in time and space, which we can measure only by sections. We can never reach the top of the ladder; for it is just as impossible for us to conceive of a beginning or an end to time and space as it is to imagine that time and space never were at all.

Thus our reasoning faculties are inadequate if we wish to express any vital truth in terms of daily language. Such vital truths are: existence, life, death, the cause of thought or the way to awaken the revelation within us. The words which our reason has concocted belong to a world where everything is measurable and contradictory (as are life and death). In fact, contradiction exists in the very thought that has coined these words. The sacred language of the letter-numbers, however, is not a product of this thought. These signs are apertures through which to glimpse the presence of the cosmic forces. What is more, they permit these forces to penetrate into our very being.

It is necessary that we understand the extraordinary dissimilarity between the language of the letter-numbers and our own language, into which the so-called translations of the Bible were made. This difference becomes strikingly evident with regard to the word *Bereshyt*, the very first sequence of letter-numbers in the Bible: 2.200.1.300.10.400. It is absurd that this should have been translated, *In the beginning (God created the heaven and the earth*). That unconceivable "beginning" abruptly thrusts the mind into the deadlock of a creed. The believer is he who dreams an unthinkable thought.

We make two fundamental errors. In the first place, our own language is an exclusive language: that is to say, if we speak the words "chair" or "yesterday" or "hot", we exclude every thought that is *not* "chair" or "yesterday" or "hot". We have thus settled our thoughts exclusively upon a certain thing or fact. But when this thing or fact is "the beginning of all things", which we cannot conceive, we do not know what we are talking about—we are simply dreaming.

The second error is to use this limiting thought in trying to perceive the totality of life; for as soon as we designate something that we do not know, we do not designate something that exists. At once, we are in the projection of our dream. We can "talk our heads off" saying words such as God, the Eternal, Supreme Being, or Universal Mind; but what we mean by those terms will never be anything more than indefinite imagery, and very mediocre and puerile at that, since it is in accordance with the limited measure of our own thought.

The result of these two mistakes is that as "believers" we tend to think of God in terms of men. We attribute to "him" thoughts, will, projects, a plan of evolution and what not. When in our thinking we relate ourselves to something which we do not know, we are, in fact, imagining something about which we are ignorant. What we need, instead of faith, is direct perception. This includes, first of all, knowledge of ourselves. Our instrument of perception being ourselves, if we do not perceive directly so as to *be* Revelation itself, why do we not "check" our instrument and detect the flaws in our functioning, instead of searching for truth with inadequate means? To discover where and what is the error: that is what truth is.

Remember, *But he turned and said unto Peter, Get thee behind me, Satan: thou art an offence unto me: for thou savourest not the things that be of God, but those that be of men* (Matt. xvi, 23). Translated into other languages, the text runs thus: *Because your thoughts are not*

the thoughts of God, but the thoughts of men (which associate themselves inseparably with continuity in existence, *Yod*).

We have often mentioned the reversal of cosmic energy from
Aleph to *Yod*. We have seen it epitomized in the historical action
of Moses. We will again witness it further on when Judas will
do what he is bidden, by becoming the instrument of *Jesus-
Aleph*'s delivery unto the world of *Yod*.

The understanding of that reversal is essential. The code of
letter-numbers will be of no avail if we do not instruct our sense-
based thought to yield to the disruptive pressure of timelessness
and to the necessity of allowing its immanence to blend with its
opposite, and still keep itself alive.

We have to remember that the only instrument of investigation that we possess is our mind. If we do not completely
understand how our mind works, this instrument will twist and
disfigure whatever of "reality" we may discover. The quality
and condition of the telescope govern the observation resulting
from its use. If there is dust on our lense, we see dark spots in the
heavens.

We have seen in the six letter-numbers of *Bereshyt* the elements
of the problem. We can now understand the *Bayt*, and *be* it
totally. But we have so far gleaned but few ideas concerning the
letter-number, *Aleph* (1)—just enough to know that we cannot
know the *Aleph*, that the *Aleph* is unknowable. If we should
pursue ideas concerning the *Aleph* following the wrong habit of
thousands of years, we shall never discover it. It is *not* a question
of finding and of understanding intellectually the creative and
timeless immanence, discontinuous and always new, having
neither past nor future, always present, in which the rhythm
of life-death is one unified whole. This *Aleph* is *in* us; but one
of the means of stifling it, of killing it, is to seek it out, to hunt
for it! There are innumerable ways of stifling and killing it. To
deny or to believe it, or to resort to alcohol or to prayers: all
these have the same disastrous effect.

Considered in its original, fundamental position, the problem is a duality—non-duality consisting of life-death *Aleph* (1),

which is intermittent, and *Bayt* (2), which is a continuing process of existence bent upon preserving its continuity. Knowing that the body is mortal, the psyche identifies itself with the continuum of existence and invents religions in order to persuade itself that it will carry on indefinitely, in the form of an immortal soul or otherwise. The psyche does not wish to understand that this belief is absurd, the "always" of duration, of time, being unthinkable.

Thus the psyche makes no distinction between what it calls the Eternal and duration. But if there is anything which transcends thought, it has nothing to do with the element of time. It is non-time. And if in that transcendence there is no time at all—nor space—then it is "happening" not only here and now, but everywhere else, no matter where or when. To project the Revelation into a morrow or into a heavenly hereafter is to imagine that, after counting to an enormous number of billions, some special number will emerge from its numerical order. Today is as good as any day, and so with a number. Piling them up will lead nowhere. To believe that Revelation took place only in the times of Abraham or of Pontius Pilate is equally mistaken.

So if, in spite of *Aleph* being within us we are in darkness and if, instead of being reborn as new beings without a past or future, we are entangled in a mediocre existence, the reason is that we prevent the *Aleph* within us from functioning. If we prevent *Aleph* from operating, then our thinking is wrong. Moreover, if we believe that the Revelation can be transmitted to us by somebody else—Abraham, Moses, Jesus or Mohammed—we are labouring under a delusion because no matter what we are told or what we have read, we shall be holding ideas about what we think someone else has experienced; these are mere projections and have nothing to do with reality.

In short, if we find what we are "looking for", it is always ourselves that we find. We must then stop searching and bring about a salutary reversal of our efforts. As a beginning, we will avoid thinking about anything that we cannot conceive of. In other words, we shall leave the mind free and simply listen to this story.

A very last reminder before going into the text: let us not build a creed upon *Aleph*. Although *Aleph* cannot be known it can be witnessed. We observe it in the fact that thought cannot think of a duration which never ends; in the fact that our everyday thought is established on a duality; and in the fact, also, that the further we investigate our own minds the deeper is the mystery of existence as such. Ultimately we come to realize that consciousness is a discontinuous phenomenon. Qabala is a training of the mind that makes it so subtle and pliable as to allow it to pass through the mysterious doorway of human genesis and enter into the sphere where life-death and existence carry on their inter-play. Jointly, on both sides, the most precious gift of life is at stake: the principle of Indetermination, which allows all that can be to become.

5

The Reading of the Text
The Creative Immanence

GENESIS CHAPTER I, I. Mistranslated, *In the beginning God created the heaven and the earth.* In the original letter-numbers this is: *Bereshyt Barah Elohim et Ha Shamaim Vay et Ha Eretz.*

Bereshyt: Containers of existences, existences in their containers. Universe containing the existences, containing its own existence. (Movement of the Universe.) Upspringing of life, intermittent pulsation invisible, not thinkable; life always new, always present, never present.

Creation! Vertiginous movement, immeasurable movement, movement that transcends all conception. In the hidden depths of movement is the secret of existence. And this movement is the custodian of all possible possibilities. Existence, projection of life, negation of existence. (Everything that exists must cease to exist.) Apparent betrayal of life. Revelation! Life-death is One. And the collision, the shock of passive resistance of the mass, the hard, the dry, the stones: blessed resistance! Without resistance there could be no birth. This is the becoming.

Thus are introduced the two partners playing against each other: *Aleph* springing from its containers, and *Yod* smitten by the "breath" of *Sheen* pressing against all that resists it so as to contain it.

Barah: Creation. Creation, violent, triumphant affirmation of the creative immanence. The surging—or revolving—action of perpetual creation gives birth to its own containers: *Bara, Bar-Aleph* means: son of *Aleph.*

Elohim: Total process through which timeless *Aleph* becomes

78

Yod which is of time. This process sets in motion the organic functions of living beings.

Existence is projected into the passive multitudes of resistance. These allow themselves or do not allow themselves to be fertilized after the manner of the living and the dead waters.

Et: If you are now thinking that you have understood the given elements of the problem, you are on the wrong track. You have only the *idea* of it, and the idea is not the thing. The problem, reduced to its essential equation, is: *pulsation of life and cosmic resistance.*

Ha Shamaim Vay Et Ha Eretz: The manifestation is twofold: there is the existence of that which contains and the life of that which is contained. Existence of the husks and the life of the kernels. External circumstances and interior life. The action of the gardener, of air, sun and water, and the life of the seed which will produce the plant, the flower, the fruit. The whole of existence is always in the grip of two forces which are heading towards a catastrophe that threatens, either through pressure of the life force from within or because of attack from the outside.

You can now see that the problem is unfolding: this interaction of existence and of life is like two players who agree to play against one another. If they were not thus associated, no game would be possible. If *Aleph* and *Yod* were not in that relationship, we would not be here talking about them. There would be nothing at all!

Existence is the continuing factor: vegetation and the animal kingdom. In all these existences, the pulsation of creative life—discontinuous, timeless—is so profoundly buried and hidden away that it seems to be absent. It seems to be absent everywhere: in the cosmos, in inter-stellar space, in the billions and billions of suns where we can neither perceive nor conceive of there being life, properly speaking. But in one form or another, even in no form at all, even engulfed and hidden, the creative immanence, active or inactive, is there. It is both in the movement and the beauty of the universe.

All this is said in the first verse of Genesis, and even much more. Yet all that is said there can never be totally divulged because of the unfathomable complexity of the Revelation. In this game between existence and life, the text already implies that whereas the fixed role of the vegetable and animal kingdom is existence-versus-life, the role of man is to change sides in the game: to be *Aleph* against *Yod*. From the amoeba up to man, all life is within the realm of continuity. Man, says the Book of Genesis is called upon to enter into that which transcends continuity and time. Reciprocally, when Elohim is entwined with YHWH, the process of life enters into existence. But all this is so difficult to grasp that for thousands of years people have read the Bible without really knowing what it means!

Genesis 1, 2. Mistranslated, *And the earth was without form, and void: and darkness was upon the face of the deep. And the Spirit of God moved upon the face of the waters.* Let us forget this translation with its "void" earth, but let us once more review the natures of the two fundamental protagonists of the game of life versus existence: Aleph and Yod.

In order to simplify the explanation of the text in the sense of its original meaning, we shall from now on refer to the two protagonists of the game of life versus existence by their names, *Aleph* and *Yod*. We will review once more their natures, for all of this is difficult to assimilate.

(*a*) The name of the so-called earth, which is Eretz, begins with *Aleph*. The *Aleph* (1) is creative immanence, timeless and immeasurable, like an intermittent spark, which our thinking cannot grasp. Were we to imagine it, we should consider the *Aleph* as a succession: being, non-being, being, non-being—or life-death, life-death, life-death. The *Aleph* appears in the first verse as one of the given elements in this Revelation. But we repeat that while the *Bayt* (2) and the *Raysh* (200) are containing elements, or containers, and accessible to our thinking, the *Aleph* (1) is only an idea in the succession of *Bayt Raysh Aleph Sheen Yod Tav*, composing the first sequence in the Bible: *Bereshyt.*

Bayt and *Raysh* are understandable, but not so *Aleph*. *Aleph* is buried in Eretz. To allow it to spring forth alive in us is *the* absolute function of every human being. In whomsoever the *Aleph* lives and functions is the very Revelation itself. *Aleph* is buried in all the containing elements—in the cosmic container-forms, the stars and the planets, etc., as well as in the container-forms of individuals. The word encompassing every variety of container is Eretz, which all translators have reduced to one word, earth.

What, then, is the aspect of these container-elements in which *Aleph* is buried? The life in them simply swarms, uncontrolled, in a state of (says the verse) "Tohu and Bohu", which is a jumble, a confusion, a hurly-burly, a chaos. It is a fantastic whirlpool of life, not limited to the planet earth, but cosmically including all that exists in the Universe. And, at "the face of its very self", in its very "deepness", that chaos is totally fecund, abundant, prolifically fertile. Such is the "darkness" referred to in the accepted translation. And such is the true meaning of the first part of the second verse concerning Eretz, the so-called earth; that in which *Aleph* is concealed.

(*b*) The so-called "heaven" in the first verse, the name of which is *Shamaim*, contains a *Yod* between two *Mem*. This sequence indicates the cosmic movement of *Sheen* acting against *Mayim*, the so-called waters: the two *Mem* (40) between which *Yod* is playing against its partner *Aleph* in the game of existence versus life. *Yod* is all we know and all that exists, and all that we can think about. Its mass, its space, its time are the mass, the space, the time, and the dwelling of all that exists. And it plays against its very destruction. And that which plays against it is the so-called Spirit of God, which is the tremendous vital energy of *Sheen* originated by *Aleph*. (The word God is the inadequate translation of Elohim, previously defined as a summing-up of *Aleph* in action and having nothing to do with the general idea of God, which is beyond thought.)

The process concerning the player *Yod* is obviously entirely different from that concerning *Aleph*. *Yod* is always, so to speak, between the hammer and the anvil. We mentioned that process already, giving the egg as an example. If the shell is not hard enough, the germ dies for lack of adequate protection; and if it is too hard, the germ dies from too much protection. Therefore *Yod* must always be in possession of two contrasting qualities; strength and softness. *Yod* must be very earnest and single-minded and yield to the delicate hint of the weakest life within it. It must be totally still, yet quick in following the movement of all that is transient. If *Yod* insists on one of these qualities against the other, what happens is a "dead death". (This expression, *Mawt-Hamawt*, will be used in a later description of Adam in Eden.)

Thus the so-called Spirit of God acts like a steam roller every time *Yod* does not play the game properly. And that action is one of the facts of life that we know best: wars, destructions, disasters of all sorts, both in the outer world and in our own inner life; our frustrations and failures; the annihilation of our achievements; and the terrible refusal of life in response to our hopes and our projects. But from these ruins, these misfortunes, rise the triumphs of ever-fertile life. In order that the new may spring forth without ceasing, must not the old, also without ceasing, be destroyed? This destructive aspect of life is essentially the activity of *Aleph*: the action of non-temporal life against the continuity of existence, with its resulting violence and despair.

6

The Light that is Life

Genesis I, 3-13. Verses 3 to 13 describe the activity of the cosmic forces that are indicated by the first three letters of the alphabet: *Aleph* (1), *Bayt* (2) and *Ghimel* (3). This activity is not that of the first three days of Creation, as all the exoteric traditions assert. Rightly understood, the text does not relate a Creation in a succession of six days, after which the divinity is supposed to have rested on the seventh day. This legend is too childish. A divinity who rests after his labour is too obviously a projection of the human mind. The succession of his labours is equally absurd. The creation of the planet Earth, in a totally empty universe, is contrary to all evidence. The appearance of the entire vegetable world on the third day, although the sun, the moon and the stars do not appear until the fourth, is the negation of all common sense. Only two courses are open to us; either we consider this whole story to be little more than a nursery rhyme, or else we seek for hidden meanings. For centuries, theologians have sought a solution to the problem without reaching a satisfactory interpretation.

One cannot satisfy the logic of pure reason and hold to the traditional meaning of the text, so, at the outset, let us resolutely forgo everything commonly thought about the Book of Genesis. The first step consists in rejecting the idea that a succession of events took place. On the contrary, everything happened at once, and verses 3 to 13 attempt to relate the activity of the forces *Aleph*, *Bayt* and *Ghimel*: that is to say, of the numbers 1, 2 and 3 acting simultaneously, and neither in time nor in space. Naturally, since our thinking is unable to "think" anything that is non-time and non-space, these verses

3 to 13 are symbolic and demand that the reader's comprehension extends beyond the symbols. They ask that he affect within himself the difficult reversal in the game of existence versus life, that he study what is said from the standpoint of *Aleph* and not from that of *Yod*. If for so many thousands of years this text has not been understood, except by the Qabala, the reason is that those who have read it have done so without bringing about this change within themselves.

We will now transcribe letter by letter (number by number) Genesis 1, 3 so familiar in its mistaken translation: *And God said, Let there be light and there was light.* In Hebrew it reads: *Va-Yomer Elohim Yehy Awr Ve-Yehy Awr.*

The first schema, *Va-Yomer* (Vav-Yod-Aleph-Mem-Raysh: 6.10.1.40.200), expresses an emanation (6) which projects *Yod* (10) and Aleph (1) in the basic attribute of matter, *Mem* (40) included in the universal container *Raysh* (200). *Yomer* is not a verb as part of speech attributed to *Elohim*'s predication but an action, an exertion or projection of energy, a doing. The two "players" are here said to be thrust into the sphere of appearances.

The second schema, *Elohim* (Aleph-Lammed-Hay-Yod-Mem: 1.30.5.10.40), is the process through which Aleph (1) by initiating a physiological movement (30) in life (5) comes into existence (10) and acquires the appearance of a metamorphosis (40) which offers resistance to life and therefore gives birth to living beings.

The third schema *Yehy* (Yod-Hay-Yod: 10.5.10) can only be translated "existence-life-existence". It expresses the coming into life (5) of a double existence (10 and 10) and thus describes the distinctive mark of organic life which is always a double process, inner and outer, of germ and shell or psyche and body.

The fourth schema *Awr* (Aleph-Waw-Raysh: 1.6.200) expresses the copulation of *Aleph* and of its physical support *Raysh*. As explained in the preceding schema it is a living energy, both outer and inner. The cabalists have always laid great stress on that symbol, both in its physical and in its metaphysical significance.

The fifth schema *Va-Yehy* is a repetition of the third. *Yehy-Va-Yehy* is an action in two proceedings from the one essence linked copulatively by *Waw*. It insists on the fact that *Awr*, which we call light, is essentially alive in a self-creative twofold mode of being. (The authors of this text would have had no difficulty in simply stating "Elohim made light" if it had been this that they had wished to say.)

The sixth schema repeats *Awr* and the reader must be very attentive when such repetitions occur in the Bible, because they always have a hidden purpose.

Awr and *Awr*: inner light and outer light. Whether intuition and perception, or heart and mind, or soul and body, whatever their names, when they come to mean something to us, inside us, when their joint action is fruitful, the Revelation is here.

Why has this twofold energy, deriving from the action of the universal life-force upon its cosmic container, been translated as "light"? The answer is that the Universe, considered as a space-time continuum, is set into motion at the maximum speed of which it is capable. According to a very ancient tradition, Genesis 1, 3 says that that maximum speed is the speed of light. Whether this statement is absolutely correct or not, scientifically, is irrelevant. Some day it may be found that the highest speed of which the Universe is capable is not only alive but that it *is* the throbbing of life throughout the entire cosmos. This speed has a number, a measure, which defines the mass, space and time of the Universe as well as its duration.

In other words, the infinite movement of *Aleph* imprints in the mass of *Raysh* the greatest speed of which *Raysh* is capable. It can be inferred that in absolutely all components the universe yields to the mighty power of *Aleph*, or again that the universe is totally permeated by *Aleph* to the point of perpetually generating it, so that *Aleph* indefinitely becomes its own son.

To reiterate in plain and simple language, Genesis 1, 3 states that, as a consequence of the interplay between the pulsating *Aleph* and the continuous existence of *Yod*, *Aleph* is copulatively (*Waw*) projected into the Universe (*Raysh*). This living process is therefore expressed in the sequence *Aleph-Waw-Raysh*, which spells the word *Awr* (pronounced *Or*), which is what we call light.

We are, here, at the origin of the tradition concerning light, which the Bible mentions a hundred times or more, including the well-known words in the Gospel of John (1, 4): *and the life was the light of man.* This, however, must be put into the present tense, along with the ensuing verse, thus: *the life* is *the light of man. And the light* shines *in darkness : and the darkness* comprehends *it not.*

This means that it is no good our merely knowing intellectually, that the life of *Aleph* is in us. You will see, as you follow the text of Genesis, that the whole question centres upon our allowing *Aleph* to spring forth within us in total freedom. In order that this may occur, and we say this again, we must cease taking sides with *Yod* and the idea of static continuity, and play the game on the side of *Aleph*. This means, of course that we must die to every minute of every day, die to every thought, to every definition of ourselves and of our supposed relationship with a God of our projection. Far from being a suicidal process, this is on the contrary a cleaning of our "house", a letting go of the mechanism of existence to which *Yod* would have us cling. It is not possible to "believe" in a Revelation and at the same time to *be* it. Believing is an escape, a refusal of it. If there is a Revelation, it exists *now*; and that "darkness" which comprehends it is forthwith made pregnant by it. But this calls for a depth of perception and a stillness of the mind which have nothing to do with neurotic revivals and their noisy emotional overflowings. The Revelation can only "take over" in us in seriousness, simplicity and silence.

7

The Light that is Darkness

GENESIS 1, 4. The beginning of this verse reads thus in Hebrew: *Veyarey Elohim Et Ha-Awr Ki-Tov.* The schemata *Et* and *Ki* having been translated in many fanciful ways according to the whims or creeds of translators, this sentence could just as well be interpreted: "and Elohim saw, because the light was good". The obviousness of such a statement would dispel the ambiguous halo of religiosity which surrounds the traditional and *God saw the light that it was good.*

The first schema *Veyarey* (*Vav-Yod-Raysh-Aleph*: 6.10.200.1) says that the impregnation (6) of the existence (10) in the universe (200) allows Aleph (1) to spring forth. Compared to *Bara* (*Bayt-Raysh-Aleph*) which in Genesis 1, 1 means "create", *Veyarey* appears as its analytical explanation.

The second schema *Elohim* has already been explained as being the process through which *Aleph* becomes *Yod* and resurrects from that material metamorphosis. Life in its oneness moves up and down, down and up, from infinite to finite, and from duration to timelessness.

The third schema *Et* (*Aleph-Tav*: 1.400) is an equivalent to our expression: "from A to Z", *Aleph* and *Tav* being the first and last letters of the alphabet. The infinite energy *Aleph* and its container's resistance *Tav* are assembled here in a synthetic view of the fact *Awr.*

The fourth schema *Ha-Awr* adds *Hay* (5), life's archetype, to the schema *Awr* (which has been explained when dealing with the preceding verse).

The fifth schema *Ky* (*Kaf-Yod*: 20.10) says that *Awr* is only considered here in its aspect as physical support of energy. *Kaf*

(20) is the archetype of *Bayt*-in-existence, 2 × 10. *Yod* (10) emphasizes that existence. (The inner light will only appear in Genesis II when the birth of man will be described not from the point of view of physical evolution but through perception of its essence.)

The sixth schema *Tov* (*Tayt-Waw-Vayt*: 9.6.2) describes the female character (9) of proliferation (6) of bodies or containers (2). *Tov* is the sempiternal function of nature indefinitely repeating its prototypes. The fact that it means "good" in colloquial Hebrew reveals the deep craving of the psyche for a static state of existence.

The second part of Genesis I, 4 is always translated: *and God divided the light from the darkness*, in spite of the fact that "God" could not have previously seen the light "that it was good" had it not been already divided from darkness. In Hebrew it reads thus: *Vayavdel Elohim Beyn Ha-Awr Ve-Veyn Ha-Hhosheykh*.

The action *Yavdel* (translated divided) *Yod-Vayt-Dallet-Lammed* (10.2.4.30) introduces in the existence (10) of containers (2) the necessary resistance to life (4) which allows them to become organic (30). The schema *Beyn* or *Veyn* (2.10.700) does not mean "divide" in Hebrew, but "between" or rather "among", and according to the code it has a far greater significance. Its letter-numbers show that 2 and 10 (containers in existence) unfold a cosmic 700 which is the first and ultimate principle at stake in the universe: the freedom of indetermination. This is granted by the action *Yavdel* to both *Awr* and *Hhosheykh*.

This last schema (*Hhayt-Sheen-Khaf*: 8.300.500) when read according to the code reveals its origin and its nature. It designates the immeasurable reservoir of undifferentiated energy (8) in relationship with the cosmic metabolism (300) and the cosmic life (500). This "darkness" is swarming with all that *could* be, and its living power transcends all human thought. From it, the action of *Yavdel Veyn*, in time, order and measure, gives birth to all that *can* become and be.

The same action of *Yavdel Beyn* upon *Awr* bestows to such

elements of *Awr* as *can* be stirred into organic motion the blessed bounty of undetermined freedom.

How, when and where this liberality is taken advantage of is explained in the following chapters of Genesis and in the text-books of Qabala. What we need to know at this point of our reading is the contradictory characters, which appear in *Yavdel*, of *Dallet* (4) and *Lammed* (30). *Dallet* expresses the resistance that any given structure opposes to that which tends to destroy it. *Lammed* is the organic movement that results from the overthrowing of obsolete structures. All organic structures have a necessary quality of resistance which deteriorates into rigidity and self-preservation. Evolution, according to Qabala, is a series of simultaneous destruction-construction of resistances, the biosphere being an interplay between structures and un-structured energies (analogically *Awr* and *Hhosheikh*).

Let us look again, from that point of view, at the schema *Tov*. translated "good" in Elohim's repetitive assertion (Gen. 1, 10, 12, 18, 21, 25): *God saw that it was good*, and again (Gen. 1, 31): *And God saw everything that he had made, and, behold, it was very good*. The words translated "very good" are *Tov-Meod*: 9.6.2-40.1.4.

Not only is 9.6.2 the building of shells (or containers, or physical supports) but 40.1.4 which qualifies that process could not express more clearly the imprisonment of *Aleph* within two resistances, 40 and 4.

These assertions must therefore be understood as indicating the powerful tendency of nature to enjoy its fructification in existence by means of a repetitive process (. . . *every living creature . . . after their kind*: Gen. 1, 21).

Let us consider by means of an example the interplay between established existence and the infinite possibilities born of life-death: as a consequence of the activity in the totality of life it so happens that in a particular place, at a particular time, a lily-of-the-valley comes into being. This flower is the maximum of life (or light) that such a place and such a time have been capable of bringing forth. So existence gloats over it and says: "Am I not beautiful? I score a point." But life answers: "Rejoice if you wish, but a lily-of-the-valley will never be anything but a lily-of-the-valley. I, life, am total and unconditioned, vast cosmic energy and movement. Out of this, anything can happen, whereas from a lily-of-the-valley, only a lily-of-the-valley can be born."

The stability of certain "living fossils" is amazing. Termites are identical with what they were during the oligocene age. Their firmly established society has indeed maintained its victory against life throughout immense geological periods. The spirit of Aleph is definitely dead in its functioning for functioning's sake. The reader of the Bible here receives a severe challenge: which of the two partners Aleph and Yod, does he wish to play for? If he associates himself with the psychological structures of his conditioning, he will build his existence (Yod) on a sense of duration and a craving for continuance—and the Revelation (Aleph) will evade him. But if he breathes the cosmic breath of life, his own "darkness" will breed the unknown which passes understanding.

Genesis 1, *5. Veiqra Elohim Le-Awr Yom Ve-Le-Hhosheykh Qara Layla (and God Called the light Day and the darkness he called Night).* This translation is too infantile to be commented upon. What the verse really explains concerns the results of *Yavdel* in both *Awr* and *Hhosheykh. Awr* becomes *Yom,* and *Hhosheykh* becomes *Layla.*

As is always the case in the Bible, a change of name expresses a complete change of form, character and condition. *Awr (Aleph-Waw-Raysh)* actually becomes something different, which is called *Yom (Yod-Waw-Mem),* when, as has been stated so often already, *Aleph* becomes *Yod.* Yom is the projection in existence of *Awr.*

Likewise *Hhosheykh* becomes *Layla (Lammed-Yod-Lammed-Hay:* 30.10.30.5). When it comes into existence, this new schema, as can be seen when decoded, expresses vividly the vital quality of that obscure (unseen) existence (10) between the organic lives (30 and 30). The *Hay* (5) which completes the schema is a reassertion of life.

Thus ends the first "days", which is not a period of time but the action of *Aleph*.

Genesis I, *6-8*. These verses apparently relate the creation of *a firmament in the midst of the waters to divide the waters which were above the firmament*. And the translation goes on to say: *and God called the firmament heaven*. (In some texts; *expanse* for *firmament*.)

It is true that *Maym* (*Mem-Yod-Mem*: 40.10.40) in colloquial Hebrew means "waters". The Qabalists (and alchemists) have always considered *Maym* as a symbol of the biochemical sphere's attributes, because analogically the waters are the natural environment for epigenesis.

Let us not forget that we are dealing with a treatise on thermodynamics. We have seen in Genesis I, I a double equation of energy as *Aleph* and *Yod* (as infinite animation and as its own physical casting). *Awr* is the equation of their symbolic wedlock (*Raysh*, 200 being the symbol of the entire cosmic physical support). We have then seen *Yavdel* as the biosphere's process which originates two trends of structures in each of the two aspects of energy, *Awr* and *Hhosheykh*. In Genesis I, 6-8, which we are now considering this entire process is seen as from the point of view of *Bayt* (2), so-called the second "day"; *Bayt* being the symbol of all containers. The protagonists, *Raysh* and *Aleph* must be expressed now as they appear in existence. But we know that *Aleph* does not possess the quality of existence in duration. Therefore its symbol must perforce be *Qof* (100) because, as we have already stated, *Qof* is symbol of cosmic *Aleph* in existence, both *Aleph* and *Yod*, blending the opposites, timelessness and time. *Raysh* and *Qof* assert their existence *Yod*. But what is the result of this wedlock? It obviously is *Ayn* (70), the principle of indetermination, which is the common stake of both parties. The equation thus formed, *Raysh-Qof-Yod-Ayn* (200.100.10.70): reads *Raquiy*, and is an energy which, not being fixed in extent, has the intrinsic quality of expansion. Energy in expansion: that is the definition of space according to Qabala. It is in expansion because, as its own container, energy cannot cope with itself. It cannot but be perpetually its own overflowing.

We are very far indeed from the "firmament" which is supposed to translate *Raquiy*, and further still from its other name "heaven" of the canonical text.

Shamaym (the schema which is translated "heaven") is simply the impact of *Sheen* (300), the cosmic metabolism, upon *Maym*. The elements of *Maym* that bear the impact are stirred by the *Ayn* (70) of *Raquiy* and they set into motion their own metabolism *Lammed* (30). The schema thus obtained is *Mem-Ayn-Lammed* which is read *Me-aal* (40.70.30) and is translated "from above", or "which were above", according to the traditional English version. The elements of *Maym* that do not bear the impact become unavailable for conversion into functional work and in that state of entropy, they return to *Tav* (400) in which the undifferentiated *Hhayt* (8) restores the resistance of *Tav* (400). The schema of that part of *Mem* is therefore: *Mem-Tav-Hhayt-Tav* (40.400.8.400). It is read *Metahhat* and is translated "from under" or "which were under".

Thus is seen the separation of the "living waters" and of the "dead waters", from the viewpoint of *Bayt* (2), said to be the "second day". It is an explanation of the mechanism by which, in Genesis I, 1, *Shamaym* is formed.

Genesis I, 9-10. We can now come to the explanation of how *Eretz* is formed. The English version is: *And God said, Let the waters under the heaven be gathered together unto one place, and let the dry land appear; and it was so. And God called the dry land Earth; and the gathering of the waters called he Seas; and God saw that it was good.* We have dealt enough with the saying, the naming and the self-congratulation of that deity. These verses explain how the energy which, through entropy, having returned to the cosmic reservoir of amorphousness, re-enters into the general cycle of life.

If we keep in mind the trajectories of *Aleph* and *Yod*, we already know that we are now going to witness *Aleph's* burial, that is, its factual deposition under earth.

The preceding verse has shown *Yod* in existence, plainly visible in *Maym* (40.10.40), held in between two biological resistances thrust into motion by Sheen (*300*) as expressed by the schema *Shamaym*. Those were the waters "above", or the biosphere.

Next we come to examine the inorganic waters "below". The Hebrew text says that they *Iqaoo* (*Yod-Qof-Waw-Waw*: 10.100. 6.6) *El Maqom Ehhad*. *Iqaoo* is the most rational and intelligent schema that can be constructed in the circumstance. Let us imagine symbolically the energy called *Aleph* falling into a *Yod* far below the organized life of the biosphere and yet proceeding along in a loop, upwards. The junction between *Yod* and *Aleph* is *Qof*, as already stated. So *Qof* is called for, appears, and with it the double *Waw* which will eventually be doubly fruitful. The second schema *El* (*Aleph-Lammed*: 1.30) need hardly be explained: *Aleph* is born again here bearing its active quality, *Lammed* (30). With the next schema *Maqom* (*Mem-Qof-Waw-Mem*: 40.100.6.40) we see *Qof* alive and fruitful taking the place of the dead *Yod* of *Maym* (100.6. in the place of 10). The last schema *Ehhad* (*Aleph-Hhayt-Dallet*: 1.8.4) means "one". It is the name of no. 1 and it expresses in a stupendous way the metaphysical disappearance from our sight of Aleph, as it actually is projected into 8 and 4.

We must add that the root of *Maqom* in Hebrew is *Qom*, to rise, to stand up, to arise. The scribes and translators, unaware of the text's meaning, could not imagine the so-called waters arising in one single upright flow of energy! In consequence, the following schemata are inverted in meaning. The schemata for *and let the dry land appear* are only two: *Vetrayeh Hayabasha*.

Vetrayeh (*Vav-Tav-Raysh-Aleph-Hay*: 6.400.200.1.5) and *Hayabasha* (*Hay-Yod-Bayt-Sheen-Hay*: 5.10.2.300.5) say that *Tav* and *Raysh* fertilized by *Vav* give birth to *Aleph* alive, and that the life *Hay* in existence *Yod* of containers *Bayt* create the very cosmic breath, *Sheen*, which is life, *Hay*.

Thus is completed the round-about journey of living energy. The beauty of its being buried in *Eretz* (*Aleph-Raysh-Tsadde*:

1.200.900) which we call earth, and which is the substance of our bodies, is its perpetual potential resurrection in us. Final *Tsadde* of *Eretz* (900) stands for beauty.

Genesis I, *11-27*. These verses further relate the facts pertaining to *Yom Shlyshy* (*Sheen-Lammed-Yod-Sheen-Yod*: 300.30.10. 300.10) translated "third day". The schema for "third": *Shlyshy*, with its two *Sheen* and two *Yod* is significant. We have seen so far the cosmic metabolism burying itself in itself in the shape (*Eretz*) of its own container. We will now see its resurrection. Genesis I, 11: . . . *let the earth bring forth grass . . . herb . . . fruit. . . whose seed is in itself. . . .* And Genesis I, 12: . . . *the earth brought forth grass . . . herb . . . fruit . . . whose seed was in itself . . .* etc. . . .

In spite of the lame translation, the two *Sheen* and two *Yod* appear here: one life is mentioned as universally bestowed, and another is endogenous. The schemata for "let the earth bring forth" are *Tadshey Ha-aretz* and the schemata for "and the earth brought forth" are *Va-Totsey Ha-aretz.*

The fundamental difference between *Tadshey* and *Totsey* has been overlooked by the translators. *Tadshey* (*Tav-Dallet-Sheen-Aleph*: 400.4.300.1) is the universal call of *Tav* (400) to the archetype of resistance *Dallet* (4), and hence the universal organic process *Sheen* (300) gives birth to *Aleph*. But *Totsey* (*Tav-Waw-Tsadde-Aleph*: 400.6.90.1) as the response of *Eretz*, manifests a 6 instead of a 4 and a 90 instead of a 300. In this difference the whole of the myth is included.

Nature's innate quality is a non-resistance, a yielding in the absolute meaning of that word: a bringing forth fruit. Therefore the Dallet of resistance is eliminated in exchange for *Waw*, and the *Sheen* is ignored for *Tsadde*.

Tsadde is not only an archetype for beauty. It also expresses the construction of forms, the building of structures, beginning with the cell, upwards. *Aleph* in *Totsey* is reborn, but either stunned or asleep or very young indeed. It will have to transcend the vegetable and the animal kingdom of *Tov*, the perpetual yielding to repetitive prototypes, until Adam learns with

Raa, traditionally said to be "evil", how constantly to destroy and rebuild his world.

Genesis 1, 14-26. The creation of the sun and moon on the "fourth day" with all the vegetation on earth developing on the "third day" clearly demonstrates that the "days" are not a succession in time.

The schema for "fourth day" is *Yom Raby-y* (*Raysh-Bayt-Yod-Ayn-Yod*: 200.2.10.70.10) in which the response of the physical supports 200 and 2 to the impetus of life reveals its adequacy (the 70 in between two *Yod* means that the germ of indeterminate freedom is held inside the double existence of organic life).

We must keep in mind that *Yom* is a coming into visible existence of *Awr*. Number 4 always expresses a resistance. We therefore understand that the sun and the moon, introduced here as luminaries, have their exact illustration in electric light bulbs utilized as resistances in a circuit in such fashion as to obtain light.

Just as *Yom* fourth brings about a resistance projected into the creation (*Awr*) of *Yom* first, the fifth begets birds and fish as living beings into the waters (above and below) of *Yom* second, and the sixth introduces all the beasts of the earth and *Adam* (male and female) into the creation of *Yom* third. There is a direct correspondence between 1 and 4, between 2 and 5 and between 3 and 6.

Cabalists must ever consider that the physical, sensorial world is an inverted symbolical projection of reality. The earth and waters, the vegetation, the fish and fowl, the animals and man, all these must be decoded so as to reveal what they actually stand for as structured living energy in multi-term analogical series.

8

An Adam and a Sabbath

WE MUST revert to certain developments in Genesis I, which had to be overlooked in a first panoramic view.

Genesis I, *22.* In this verse *Elohim* blesses the "great whales", all the creatures that move in the waters and every "winged fowl". The blessing is *Yebarekh* (*Yod-Bayt-Raysh-Kaf*: 10.2.200. 500). The whales are *Tanynym* (*Tav-Noun-Yod-Noun-Mem*: 400.50.10.50.40) and the pleonastic winged birds are *Oof-Kanaf* (*Ayn-Waw-Phay—Kaf-Noun-Phay*: 70.6.800-20.50.800).

That blessing is the bestowal of cosmic life (500) to all that lives in the waters. The particular spelling of the schema *Tanynym* expresses a double life (50 and 50) born out of 400, and *Oof-Kanaf* (literally the bird-wing) expresses a fleeting uncertainty born out of 800, and alive in 800. And thus ends that which is accomplished by *Yom* fifth, the no. 5 being that of life.

Genesis I, *24. Eretz*, the earth, is mentioned in this verse, as the third Element, after air and water (fire, *Esh* will appear much later, in Genesis II, with *Esha*, the woman, its feminine).

Genesis I, *26.* In this verse is the creation of man. Its serial number, 26 is that of *YHWH*, sometimes called *Yahveh*, sometimes Jehovah, and, in the English Bible "The Lord". We will deal later with that schema. It is spelt *Yod-Hay-Waw-Hay* ($10+5+6+5=26$), and its first appearance will occur in Genesis II. The creation of man in a verse bearing the number 26 is a prefiguration of the *YHWH*, which has hitherto not been mentioned. Man does not appear here as the exclusive product of the earth, but as proceeding from the *Elohim* which, as we know, is the vital process of the *Aleph* in action. The text which has been translated, *Let us make man in our own image, after our likeness*, actually reads approximately thus (we will not follow it here letter-number by letter-number): From the living process of *Aleph* in its cosmic body-container springs forth a factual life upsetting the mechanical repetitions of nature (where every pattern is a fixed prototype). Here an Adam is created who is in contact with the powerful movement of the Universe, and in whom every possibility is latent.

"Adam" is *Aleph immersed in blood*, but this blood is not "all-absorbing"; it can become "cosmically fruitful", which means that the human body can come to radiate cosmic energy. The schema for man (*Adam*) is *Aleph* (1), *Dallet* (4), *Mem* (40 or 600). The fact that *Mem* final can be 40 (i.e. resistance) and can leap to 600 (i.e. cosmic fertility) indicates the vast range of possibilities in man. The true vocation of mankind is this transfiguration of 40 into 600. The text goes on to say that Adam can be considered as a living shadow, or image, of the Elohim: given the potential of greater power of resistance than any other being, he can become the receptacle of the greatest intensity of life on this planet. (In a certain respect, we can see this illustrated today wherever men are being trained to withstand the strain of living in rockets, beyond gravitation, on the floor of the oceans, in the antarctic icefields, or to test their physical and psychological resistance in all kinds of competitions.)

Genesis 1, 27 says that *Adam* is created male and female; *Zakar* and *Neqivah*. In the letter-numbers which express this fact, *Zakar* (7.20.200) and *Neqivah* (30.100.2.5) we can see a relationship between the sexes which can well come as a surprise for the reader. Whereas *Zakar* does not possess the capacity by which all possible possibles can come into existence, in *Neqivah* the cosmic *Aleph* is active. This theme is so important in the development of the allegory that it must be explained at once.

The letter-numbers which designate the male (*Zakar*) are 7 constricted by containers that are both factual (20) and cosmic (200). The number seven is familiar to us being that of a state of transition: the seventh note of a scale is constantly tending towards a new octave; a seventh chord in music is a means of modulation into a new key. The number 7 is potentially open to anything which may happen to alter a previously established pattern. *Eretz*, as we have seen in the third "day" of Genesis I, 11-12, responds with a yielding of the cosmic life and produces beauty and an infinite variety of vegetation though each species is limited to the capacity of its own seed.

Whereas *Eretz* is thus enclosed in its natural repetitive process, *Adam's* blood is open to every transfiguration. For over and beyond *everything that creepeth upon the earth*, which can only develop *after his kind* (Gen. I, 25), *Adam*—as mankind, both male and female—is given a special "blessing". This blessing receives a different response from man and woman. The man (7.20.200) is constantly being upset by and upsetting history, driven unconsciously by his inner 7 towards an ideal cosmic 200; whereas the woman (50.100.2.5) is forever reshaping the 50 and 100 with the aim of safeguarding the home (2.5).

In order that *Aleph* should be born into human society, the passive female side of *Adam*, obviously, must transform itself and rise above the female "containing element" (the body). Until this has happened, the activity of the male will only be chaotic agitation. The theme of the necessary transformation of the feminine is very important in the Bible. We shall meet it again in the feminine types of *Esha*, Hhevah, Sarah, Rebecca and Rachel, etc., .. up to Mary, mother of Jesus. All these are symbolical personifications of what women must learn to become. It is unfortunate that inadequate translations have prevented women from grasping the truth concerning themselves as it is set forth in the Book of Genesis. Thus women allow themselves to be misled into allowing the male—in such fatuous roles as a high priest of racism waving the Bible, or some head of state invoking divine vengeance in a "holy war"— to exert every possible pressure to persuade all humankind that "God" is a "He", with "his" code of morals, "his" wars, etc., etc.

The Bible, from beginning to end, in every instance where

the transformation of woman is stated and taught, will never be truly understood until the transformation has become a reality alive and active in humanity. If popular thinking has been content that one woman should have been transformed in such fashion as to have become the "Mother-of-God", it is an evasion, a fantasy, a flight from reality. The lesson to be learned from the text we have just considered is far more profound and is to be lived in the here and now.

Genesis II, *1-3*. We read in the translations of these verses that thus creation is finished, that on the seventh day Elohim ended the work which he had made and rested on the seventh day, and that he blessed and sanctified that day because he rested from his work.

Of the many complex schemata of these verses we will only examine the following:

Yshbot (*Yod-Sheen-Bayt-Tav*: 10.300.2.400) translated "he rested".

Yom-Hashby-y (*Yod-Waw-Mem—Hay-Sheen-Bayt-Yod-Ayn-Yod*: 10.6.40-5.300.2.10.70.10) translated "day seventh".

Ybrakh (*Yod-Bayt-Raysh-Khaf*: 10.2.200.500) translated "blessed".

Yqdesh (*Yod-Qof-Dallet-Sheen*: 10.100.4.300) translated "sanctified".

According to the code, we see that the "resting" is a deep penetration of 300 into 400; the schema for seventh, shows that the life (5) of 300, in its physical support (2) is at rest because the 70 by which its influence is brought to bear is seen to exist in 10.70.10. According to these numbers, the "blessing" and the "sanctifying" express the fact that the universe is autonomous and free. The schemata concerning no. 7 says that the universal life is satisfied in that which exists (the infinite is satisfied in the numbers that support it physically), because 7 in existence (70) is satisfied by the very existence of all that is. In 70 is a motion which maintains every possible possibility of unfoldment.

So we are not in the least obeying a biblical precept when we think that we have to be bored on Sundays or Sabbath and do

THE CIPHER OF GENESIS

nothing. The "blessing" of no. 7 is meant to liberate in us some potential hidden faculty. We can use a day of leisure to find out whether some quality exists in us or not. If we can use it to discover a latent talent or a useful hobby, to explore nature, or in any way to expand our inner or outer horizons, then we will have a Sunday or a Sabbath in the true spirit of the Bible. Churches, synagogues, temples or mosques, their ceremonies and their prayers, have nothing to do with the true Sunday or the true Sabbath.

The "blessing" and the "sanctifying" of the number 7 also have a definite meaning. Both words, in their original letter-numbers, signify joyfulness, a sense of extraordinary freedom, a life open to anything that may come to it. And the blessing which is granted is the sanctification of freedom. This is the immeasurable joy of yielding, of letting be, of not imposing any psychological structure upon anyone. From that point of view, we can receive the "blessing" and "sanctifying" of life every day in the week.

A SUMMARY OF THE SEVEN DAYS

The first and foremost thing to keep in mind is that the "days" of creation describe a simultaneous, perpetual, and ever-present action of the 3 archetypes *Aleph*, *Bayt* and *Ghimel*, of their corresponding *Dallet*, *Hay*, *Waw* and of *Zayn* the seventh. They describe the autonomous life and movement of the universe.

Awr (*Aleph-Waw-Raysh*) is symbolically the copulation of the discontinuous and unthinkable *Aleph* and of its cosmic container *Raysh*. Its result is the greatest speed of which the universe is capable. It is identified with light.

Yehy Awr Va-Yehy Awr ("let there be light and there was light") when read letter by letter is actually: "the life of all existence (double), consequence of *Aleph* in copulation with the universe".

Awr is *Tov*, i.e. conditioned and repetitive. It is a structured

100

energy distinct from *Hhosheykh*, which is the life of undifferentiated primordial energy.

Awr coming into existence becomes *Yom*. *Hhosheykh* becomes *Layla*.

The verb *Yqra* must not be translated "said". There is no divinity using a vocabulary. *Yqra* is an emanation of the two partners in the cosmic game of life-death and existence: *Aleph* and *Yod*.

Aleph is in everything and everything is in *Aleph*. *Bayt* (physical support) is with everything and everything is with *Bayt*. *Ghimel* (movement) is energy and all energy is *Ghimel*.

The container *Eretz* engenders nature in its beauty according to what it is but not according to what the cosmic breath is.

Visible reality is an inverted symbol of an invisible reality.

Yom seventh is the autonomy of the universe. It is autonomous because it has the capacity of allowing *Aleph*'s resurrection. Had it not that capacity, it would not exist.

ADDENDUM

The words (Gen. 1, 5, 8, 13, 19, 23, 31) *And the evening and the morning were the* (first, second, third, etc. . . .) day contradict my assertion that those days are simultaneous and not consecutive.

The schemata concerning those passages are: *Ve-Yehy Ayrev Ve Yehi Voqer. Yom (Ehhad,* etc. . . .).

The schema *Yehy* is the one that is translated "let there be" (light) and "there was" (light); it is here translated "were". Such variations indicate that the necessities of a rational grammar must not be considered. That schema cannot be translated: it propounds synthetically the concepts Existence-Life-Existence and suggests the springing forth into existence of something alive.

The schemata *Ayrev* and *Voqer (Ayn-Raysh-Vayt—Vayt-Qof-Raysh)* when read in succession 70.200.2 - 2.100.200 (and if it is remembered that *Yom* is *Awr* appearing into existence) clearly reveal a rhythm, an alternation, a circuit which from the indeter-

101

minate 70 in the cosmos (200) affects the individual 2 and from 2 returns to 200 through the mediatory *Qof* (100).

This, which we should venture to call an umbilical rhythm, pertains to the first six letter-numbers and not to no. 7. It is apparent in the order of the world, in nature and its seasons and in everything which is only *Tov*. In mankind groping in strife and blood towards its indistinct maturity it does not exist. He, however, who would live that rhythm in accordance with the cosmic breath of life would be highly benefited by it. Let us read the text as it is written, however mistranslated: "and the evening and the morning" (are a day). The day is meant to begin in the evening. When night begins to fall, he (Adam) retires and purifies his body and soul. During the day he has met many difficulties; many problems, many uncertainties have assailed him. Now he collects his thoughts, he stills his passions, he communes with himself and with the essence of life, and as *Hhosheykh* comes upon him and in him, the impersonal creative powers can gradually unfold. That is *Ayrev*, the 70.200.2. Then, in the morning, the *Voqer* 2.100.200 can set out again from the house, the *Bayt*, and refreshed by *Qof*, again meet and renew the challenge of *Raysh*.

He who, in the evening of his life, would find the freshness of newly lived morning, that man would be a man of *Qabala*.

9

An Arising

GENESIS II, 4-6: *Here are the generations of Shamain and of Eretz, created the Yom that YHWH Elohim made them. And the plants of the fields were not yet on Eretz and the herbs of the fields had not yet grown because Yod-Yod-Elohim had not caused it to rain on Eretz and there was no Adam to cultivate. But Ad arose from Eretz and watered the whole face of Adamah.**

Because it is prescribed in the Jewish religion never to pronounce YHWH, this schema is sometimes reduced to Yod-Yod and always uttered *Adonaï* (The Lord). Thus, in order to avoid desecrating whatever the formula YHWH stands for, it is interpreted as designating an anthropomorphous deity: in English, the Lord God.

YHWH: 10.5.6.5, Existence-Life-Copulation-Life, expresses in existence the two lives (that of the container or shell or physical support, and that of the contained or germ or inner life) that fertilize each other. This double impregnation can only occur in Man and as long as it does not occur YHWH is immanent but unborn. We will often refer to this schema. For the time being, in Genesis II, 5-6, Adam has not yet appeared. We will see him created in verse 7 before all the animals.

The impulse to his creation is given (Gen. I, 6) when *Ad* is born of *Eretz* and waters *Adamah* (translated "there went up a mist from the earth . . ."). This fact symbolizes the endogenous quality acquired by *Eretz* on *Yom* seventh.

The point of view of Genesis II is here already apparent. It does not belong to a Yahvic tradition different from and in-

* The whole meaning of those verses is in the schemata according to code. I therefore refrain from quoting the traditional English text.

consistent with the Elohimic tradition of Genesis I (as has been stated by scholars). It describes the universal life-energy as seen from inside, from its essence, and no longer through its evolutionary aspect. The essence is included in the appearance, the beginning is in the end and the end is in the beginning.

Hence the schema *Ad* (*Aleph* and a resistance, *Dallet*). *Aleph* immersed in the non-resistant Eretz springs forth with a resistance that does not belong to the limited response of *Eretz* to the cosmic breath, and it "waters" (fertilizes) that *Eretz* and transfigures it in such fashion as to give it the status of *Adamah*, (translated "ground") the feminine of Adam.

This is a good example of how, in literal Hebrew and in its translations, the text loses its meaning. There is no contradiction between Genesis I where *Adam* is born at the final stage of an evolutionary process and Genesis II where he is born previous to all other living beings.

The essential conclusion of Genesis I, 5 (YHWH-Elohim "had not caused it to rain") is that the planet Earth is expected to have in itself the capacity of transmuting its substance. Genesis I, 6 (the going up of *Ad* as the creation of *Adamah*) proves that it has indeed that capacity. Hence, in Genesis I, 7, man *can* be created because it is ascertained that the substance of which he is made (*Aafar*: 70.80.200 translated "dust", of *Adama*) sets into indeterminate motion (70) the lowest strata of energy (80) in the cosmos (200).

This so-called "dust" (symbolic of crumbled rocklike rigidity) leads us by means of its letter-numbers to the realization that *Eretz* is not only the Earth. This schema stands for all cosmic bodies and for every aspect of their components, from their simplest chemical elements up to their highest biological aggregates.

10

The Adam and the Garden of Eden

GENESIS II, 7. *YHWH-Elohim* forms *Adam* of the "dust" of *Adamah* and breathes the breath of life into his nostrils.

When all these schemata are read according to the code we see that the letter *Pay* or *Phay* (80) appears in "dust", "breathes", "nostrils" and that *Sheen* (300) appears in "breath". The result of the operation is *Adam* becoming a living *Nefesh* (50.80.300). No. 80 stands for all the undeveloped strata of energy. It is given life in *Adam* by *Sheen* (300), the cosmic metabolism. Here the text leaves us in doubt as to whether this Adam, this allegorical personage, created without any connection with evolution and indeed without any past, personifies an individual or the whole human race.

The truth is that this Genesis, this creation of a complete Adam, has not yet taken place—although it may now be in process of becoming. We can begin to understand this allegory when—rather than imagining it as a mere myth of our remote past—we see that, potentially, the complete Adam can come into being within us *now*. Adam is seeking birth, but we stifle it every day in its womb. Now that we know that the mature Adam does not yet exist, let us see what happens in the Garden of Eden, so often referred to with such childish imagery.

Genesis II, 8-9. These two verses describe the Garden of Eden. Verses 10 to 14, in which are mentioned four rivers, are not as important as the rest. In verse 15 *Adam* is put into Eden. These verses raise three fundamental questions.

First: Why in this chapter is Adam created before the animals, while in chapter 1 he was created, logically, at the top of the evolutionary scale?

Second: To what cosmic forces, to what aspect of life, does the famous Garden of Eden correspond, and where is it located?

Third: Why is it said in Genesis II, 8, *and there* (in the Garden) *he put the man whom he had formed*, and later, in Genesis II, 15, (he) *took the man and put him into the Garden of Eden* . . .? Is this repetition simply a copyist's error?

The replies to these questions concern each and every one of us. Of all the beings living on this planet, man is the only one who, according to the Book of Genesis, must not be defined. We are here at the very core of Genesis: the birth of our pre-natal humanity. Imagine a primal germ of life which, throughout a lengthy series of evolutions, has developed functions of perception, of assimilation and of action. It has passed through successive mutations and given birth to more and more highly evolved species.

We can consider each animal species as being a fixation within physiological limits. This fixation, this halt in development, is an accumulation of experience that is called instinct. Instinct is an indefinite repetition of the same gesture, with a reduced margin of possible modifications. All the animal species of the Book of Genesis are considered as being the lateral branches of the tree of life, of which man occupies the innermost part, the core, in an upward surging motion of the very heart of the trunk.

Genesis is quite clear in saying that man did not descend from anything, not even a monkey. Everything which did not become Adam, whether monkey, flea, fish, or elephant, came to a halt at one level or another of evolution and shot out a branch which ends where it began. Consequently, each species is compelled to exist in a milieu which varies only to a slight extent. If the milieu alters beyond the species' capacity of adaptation, then the species dies. None of the animal species is capable of radically modifying its milieu. Each species carries on indefinitely within its limited means of survival; and when these means become inadequate, the disappearance of the species seems to leave Nature totally indifferent. For the genus *Homo*, however, the situation is completely different. Man is motivated by extraordinary violence. Our century alone, with its two overwhelming world wars, the folly of which is evident, has seen the disappearance of more empires than history ever recorded and has traced millions of miles of new frontiers which have no chance of permanent survival. Yet even this wholesale destruction and change has had a lesser impact upon the human psyche than the relentless onslaught of science upon our notions about the universe, the constitution of matter, and the nature of our own faculties. Our shocked and bewildered minds seek refuge in a permanent truth, but the how and where of the search elude us. The Book of Genesis suggests a threefold approach to this quest: a vision of the interior world (which will answer my first question); a perception of the exterior world (which will answer my second question); and the understanding of the world, which deals with the structure of the psyche, which will answer my third question.

Concerning the first question, note that Genesis II differs from Genesis I in that it is the interior vision of what Genesis I describes from an exterior viewpoint. This vision is interior because, as we have already said, YHWH is the vital process of Elohim, which has plunged into the interior of existence (seen as continuity): into its temporal and spatial life. This incarnation has set human destiny in motion. This incarnation is *a germ which does not halt at any point of evolution*. This germ is, then, anterior in origin to all the latest branches. Adam is the first-born, which means that he is never allowed to be "born" in the sense that the birth of a pattern is a fixity in a fixed setting.

The second question is: Just what is the Garden of Eden? It can be seen by reading, one by one, all the letter-numbers which describe it, that this is one of the most dangerous places in the whole world: *Gan-Eden*: *Ghimel-Noun—Ayn-Dallet-Noun*: 3.700-70.4.700. The numbers 70 and 700 are those of the destruction of obsolete structures. In fact, life—understood totally—is, in Genesis, repeatedly said to be life-death. The life to which

107

Adam is called is a series of destructions and new beginnings. Allegorically, life is "saying" all the time that this "germ" of humanity must always be prevented from achieving perfect protection and shelter. If ever it should find a fixed refuge, a comfortable stability, it would settle down lazily into a sub-human species; it would become one of these side-shoots on the tree of life. Reflect for a moment how certain tribes have remained undeveloped on account of a too pleasant or a too severe climate, or even from physiological or psychological causes. Thus, as they have become fixed in their mode of living, their faculty of adaptation has ceased to function and they are totally overwhelmed if they come into contact with the maelstrom of life in the twentieth century.

Let us consider now the phrase (in Genesis II, verse 9), *the tree of knowledge of Tov and Raa*, translated good and evil. All the Hebrew words relating to this tree (such as *gan, beeden, meqaddam*) convey intense movement. In fact, it is a whirlwind destroying all that is obsolete, as well as all accumulations, which must constantly be swept away by the totality of life that is creative and always new. This concept becomes clear to us when we realize that, in reading the Bible as we know it, the word *Tov* according to its letter-numbers (*Tav-Vav-Vayt*: 400.6.2) expresses the continuity of existence to which we cling as "good", and the word *Raa* (*Raysh-Ayn*: 200.70) that which upsets our static habits of living is translated "bad".

In spite of ourselves, the meaning of our true name of Adam is safeguarded. It is preserved in all that abolishes rigid, exclusive habits of thought and identification, as in nationalism, sectarianism and racism, etc. All this crystallization of thought and attitude courts disaster because it is the wrong way to play the game of living. So here is the answer to my third question: Genesis II, 8 is not read correctly. In this verse it is not *Adam* but the name *Adam* that is put in Eden so as to safeguard it.

The psychological structure of society teaches us to play against life, on the side of fixed continuity of existence, as if it did not wish the floods of life to reach us. And yet what *life* continually proposes is that we ride the waves, swift and overwhelming as they are.

Naturally, in order to play the game fully, we have to die and to be reborn every instant. That is, we have to accept the death of a Rabbi called Jesus in accordance with its original intended meaning—as a symbol for the way of life-death, and not as a substitute for our yielding to this intermittent pulsation in our own daily lives.

11

The Adam within the Gan Eden

THE ALLEGORY of this Adam in this "garden" Eden, *Ayn-Dallet-Noun*: 70.4.700, is very complex and difficult to understand. One must examine it very carefully and patiently and not advance until one has assimilated it step by step. The garden east of Eden is: *gan beeden meqaddam* (Mem-Qof-Dallet-Mem: 40.100.4.40 or 600), and its letter-numbers give such precise information concerning it that no doubt is possible. This purely symbolic garden is ahead of and beyond us, in anticipation of Adam. It is characterized by the greatest instability imaginable. The "germ" Adam is to be thrown into a state of great activity, a whirlwind which will never give him time to "fossilize" or to stay fixed in any time or circumstance.

The substance of this garden is named Adamah and life (YHWH-Elohim) causes this substance to bring forth, symbolically, everything that can stimulate the senses and awaken the appetite of Adam: *every tree that is pleasant to the sight, and good for food* (Gen. II, 9) and, in the middle, the two famous trees—of life, and of "good and evil". The significance of this symbolism is quite logical. As stated above, what is placed in this garden is the germ, the essence, of the human being as formulated in this book. The germ of humanity can never totally come to rest, never completely become static. This germ is an essence, a movement, a dynamism constantly projected ahead of itself— which, so to speak, never overtakes itself. Thus, although this germ is neither masculine nor feminine, here in the "garden" it possesses all the masculine characteristics and none of the feminine. The feminine of the life-germ is Adamah, from whom spring the remarkable trees in question.*

Thus, symbolically, the essence of Adam in Eden is masculine in character, and the feminine element within him is the substance of Adamah from which arises everything that is capable of developing man sensorially. You will see that this fact is important. In the midst of this sensorial development in Adam, in the very heart of it, are the two "trees" similar in appearance: for the tree of "life" is that of life-death, the non-continuous pulsation of life; and the tree of "good and evil", on another level, is the tree of *Tov-Raa*, *Tov-Raa*, the tree of fixation-destruction, fixation-destruction. The latter dominates every phase of this Adam's life and every aspect of the institutions and societies man has created. In short, the tree of life is that state in which the full pulsation of life can be attained at Adam's maturity. The other tree is that state in which Adam, not yet mature, not yet really born (the condition of Humanity at present), is caught in a continuous series of catastrophes. Everything that Adam wishes to build, whether in himself or outside of himself, crumbles to pieces.

Since Adam, at this stage of the allegory, is in a pre-natal state, the tree of life is not yet accessible to him. It is equally evident that if this human embryonic form, merely a potentiality and without substance other than that of Adamah, should set into motion the whole mechanism of *Tov-Raa*, with its chain of destruction, he would die, instantly crushed by what he had provoked. He would die, says the text, *Mawt Hamawt*: a *dead* death (without resurrection).

The allegory now shows life in its attempt to define the femininity in Adam's nature, to discover a womanliness different from the animal-female quality. Here, as usual, the text is mistranslated and misunderstood. First of all, notice the succession of ideas: if you eat of this tree, you will be annihilated.

---

* Notice how the symbols are sometimes interchangeable in the Bible. But we also frequently see them classed in the categories of masculine and feminine: as, for instance, fire, blood, wine (masculine) and water, earth, bread (feminine).

Tov is missing as long as Adam is alone: this volatile germ must be given flesh and continuity or, in other words, this embryo that is to develop must become incarnate. For this to come about, Adam must have a partner *against* him. This is the exact meaning of the text. Here again, we find the notion of a partner *against*; for man must learn to play his role and woman hers, in this partnership of life-existence against (and for) each other!

Adam now must pass a test to prove himself deserving of this partner. He must demonstrate that he has advanced far enough in the evolutionary scale to merit human incarnation. This is the test: YHWH-Elohim creates all the animals and shows them to Adam, *to see what he would call them* (Gen. II, 19). Adam looks at them, one species after another, and names them all. Each species is exactly what Adam calls it. Just what does all this mean, the "naming" and this being named? The reply is illuminating: Adam recognized each species as being an off-shoot from his own central trajectory. We know now that this is true, embryologically. The human foetus passes through all the phases of evolution in the course of its development. Adam, in placing the various species sees his own embryonic past and declares: I see nothing which is altogether like me. Thus, Adam has passed his test; for he no longer identifies himself with the animal phase of his evolution. Consequently, he is ready for incarnation.

This coming to birth takes place in Genesis II, 21-22. Unfortunately, our translations relate the childish story of Adam's sleep and of a woman being formed from one of his ribs. Is the extraordinary popularity of this interpretation through so many centuries due to its stupidity, or have its symbols a psychological attraction that could be explained through analysis? In the text, as we learn to read it, there is no "sleep" and no "rib". The germ Adam is immersed in *Tardamah*, which is an incarnation in its cosmic sense (Adamah being its living reality as human flesh); and the absurd rib is *Tsalaa*: namely, the womanliness of that incarnation, animated by a dynamic movement.

In other words, these two symbolic beings, man and woman,

are supposed to be free of their animal past, accumulated in the course of previous evolution. They are supposed to be free from instinctual, repetitive automatisms. This past is no longer active within them. This is what *Adam* says in Genesis I, 23. The name of this woman (spelled *Aleph-Sheen-Hay*) is pronounced *Esha*: *Esha* is the feminine element of cosmic fire, inasmuch as she springs from *Esh* (*Aleph-Sheen*) fire. Notice the spelling of *Eesh* for man: (*Aleph-Yod-Sheen*). *Adam* discovers this, his new name. (The addition of *Yod* to the name of fire indicates that this "fire" comes into existence in man.) A remarkable feature of these ideograms is that *Esha* does not really exist although she is alive (she has no *Yod* but has the *Hay* of life). The fire, *Esh*, from which she proceeds, has neither life nor existence. It is a pure archetype *Aleph-Sheen*. As to *Eesh*, the man, he has the *Yod* of existence but no *Hay*: he is not really alive. When we deeply investigate the notions, existence and life, we can discover that those schemata are an excellent and well-observed description of what our humanity actually is.

Verses 21 and 22 of Genesis II show how Esha is formed.

(*a*) The so-called sleep of Adam is a marvellous event, the reflected action of which is seen in the sleep of the newborn child. Compared to every other species where the newborn animal is automatically set into motion by an accumulated knowledge, the human being is born to learn; and his *not-knowing** is in proportion to his evolutionary development and tends to create the greatest possible intensity of life.

(*b*) Adam's consciousness is now freed. It leaves him and plunges into *Tardamah* (deep sleep). This schema is *Tav-Raysh* (400.200) and *Damah*, the feminine of blood. *Tav* (400) is the total resistance of life's physical support (the universe) and *Raysh* is the total organic process of universal life. We can translate that "deep sleep" symbolically by saying that in it Adam's blood is mated with the highest power of cosmic energy. Then, into this now pregnant flesh a double life is projected. The

* i.e. freedom from the animal instinct and influence of the accumulation of the past.

extraction of a rib has no connection with the cabalistic meaning of the text. The schema for rib is a shadow to which is added 70: it is the opening of all possible possibilities for man.

(c) Next YHWH-Elohim "builds" (*Yod-Vayt-Noun* final: 10.2.700) that fragment, that is, relates it to the tremendous cosmic 700. It results in a separation as if two rooms were separated by a partition or in the manner of one cell that divides and makes two; but the two parts are motivated by the same movement!

(d) The concluding phase of the operation consists in the closing of the reservoir from which the new life was taken.

Adam coming to himself, whoever and wherever he is today, and whatever his name, knows neither *Eesh* nor *Esha*, the archetypes of an *Adam* in whom Dam (the blood) is transmuted from 4.40 to 4.600.

We wonder if one must of necessity be a cabalist to understand this language or if it has a chance of being heard more widely. We will again endeavour to describe the mutation of Dam from 4.40 to 4.600.

We know that Adam is a schema for the human being. It indicates that *Aleph*, the pulsating creativeness of life-death, is within him, struggling so as not to drown in the absorption of Dam, 4.40. The earth, as *Adamah*, claims that blood as belonging to it. It says, mythically: I, Adamah, am your mother and spouse; you, my husbandman, are kin to me: you are earth.

If we accept this proposition and live accordingly, the *Aleph* in us suffers death by suffocation, just as it is buried in *Eretz* where nature continuously repeats its prototypes, each according to its species.

But the Hebraic myth states that YHWH-Elohim has breathed in man the *Sheen* (300) which is the organic movement of the whole universe (Gen. II, 7). This develops into the well-known dispute between YHWH and the earth as to whom the blood belongs.

YHWH's point contended for in argument is founded on a basic postulate of Qabala: the unity of energy and of its contradictory aspects as spirit and matter, good and evil, high and low, etc. They coalesce in the synthetic formula *Yod-Hay-Waw-Hay* where their two lives fertilize each other.

What has just been described is seen as from within cosmic forces in their relationship one with another. It is not by any means the description of a caveman descended from a pre-anthropoid type. This is a story at once abstract yet concrete, allegorical yet real, inspired yet rational. If one really wishes to comprehend it, one must receive it at the highest level of in-telligence. Immaturity becomes little short of criminal when it persists in devitalizing the mighty sweep and content of the Book of Genesis, and when its comprehension inflicts unjusti-fiable dogmas in the name of religion.

Genesis II, 24 is so little understood that certain exegetists maintain that it is an interpolation: *Therefore shall a man leave his father and mother, and shall cleave unto his wife: and they shall be one flesh.* We can set aside this translation which debases this verse in subservience to certain social interferences in con-jugality (such as alleging divorces to be against the will of "God", etc.). After having said that Adam and Esha are bound towards a new life, this verse does not in any way say that they are "one flesh", but that they join in the common action in favour of a containing element, psychological and physio-logical, which must express the cosmic movement of life as well as the resistance to it.

Verse 25 goes on to say *not* that they are naked and un-ashamed, but that Adam (he is not mentioned as Eesh) and his Esha both incorporate the number 70, which is the realization of all the possible possibilities. The letter-numbers go on to explain that this no. 70, which is the source of all that lives, is enclosed, submerged, in the "waters" (for, as you remember, all existing life begins in the water element). The end of this verse 25 states that Adam and his Esha, being enclosed as they are now in an envelope of great resistance, seem to have lost their cosmic life. We will presently see that Nahhash, the ser-pent, gives life back to Esha.

In concluding here this brief reading of chapter II, it is of interest to infer from it that it contains a description of the vital biological process through which life comes into existence. It also shows the primordial importance of the role the woman must play in the engendering of the human being.

But we all have, in varying degrees, both masculine and feminine elements in us. Whether we be men or women, we must all be Adam; and we should all learn to know what is the feminine—especially psychologically—within us. As long as the static, conserving element within us does not yield to the up-springing of cosmic fire that burns away the past and its false revelations, we shall maim the life within us and continue to go begging at the doors of religion for a knowledge which will escape us.

12

What is God?

WITH THE eating of the apple, we are reaching the story which, for centuries, has been one of the world's best-known tales. Ever since the Christian religion incorporated this narrative from the archives of an ancient Semitic people, long after its original significance had been lost, the story has always produced a sensation. No fairy tale has ever been able to compete with the talking serpent, or the enchanted garden, or the moral tree with its apples of good and evil—far more evil than good, according to the exoteric traditional interpretation, in which we delude ourselves into seeing good as evil, and evil as good.

In the preceding chapter we did not wish to enter into the incongruities that appear in the translation of this text, for we wished to deal first with what is most meaningful in the Garden of Eden. It has extraordinary import. In this present epoch (we write in the nineteen-sixties), we are approaching a turning-point of history at such speed that the full content of this message must be understood, and lived, if there are to be "new" men and women such as these of which the world is desperately in need. The Book of Genesis (Genesis means "birth") indicates what we must do to be born afresh, to be "new".

Each one of us has a choice to make and may do so freely. The choice is this: we can, if we wish, live after the manner of the animal species, which ceased to advance in the scale of evolution and continued to live within the limits of their con-ditionings, and the accumulation of their inherited automa-tisms, confined to strictly limited forms. Most of the time, we limit our conception of what we are by the patterns with which we fill our minds: *our* culture, *our* way of life, *our* traditions, *our* morals, *our* imitations, *our* ways of thinking inherited from the past, which we seek to carry into the future. By maintaining all these attitudes—with the help of our environment, our churches and our schools—we are actually stifling and killing the human-being-to-be which waits within us.

We are apparently trying to settle down into a prehuman sub-species. One thing is sure: we are not Adam, neither are we Eesh and Esha. We are rejecting the Revelation. Our righteousness and religiosity are hypocrisy. This is one choice, the easy one. In that choice, men will go on debasing womanhood, strip-teasing them for the purpose of sexual gratification, denying them equality, exploiting them or subjugating them, and imposing an exclusively male government on the world. Reciprocally, by devious means, women will take their revenge by exploiting man's ambitions and vanity. And they will *grab*. This state of affairs is *pre-* or rather *sub*-human.

The other choice means breaking with all this because one sees that it is already obsolete. One must then reject all the psychological conditioning which is forced upon us by society, by tradition, by a projection from the past. Such a choice is not easy. It is difficult to understand, let alone to live. Yet only this choice can transmute the Revelation of the Bible into living reality.

Let us now consider some of the incongruities in the accepted narratives concerning the Garden of Eden. Why did the so-called God need to plant a tree giving the knowledge of "good and evil", in a garden whose only inhabitants were forbidden to eat of it? For whom, then, did he plant that tree? He planted all the trees for the nourishment of man. Yet we read: *We may eat of the fruit of the trees of the garden: But of the fruit of the tree which is in the midst of the Garden, God hath said. Ye shall not eat of it* (Gen. III, 2-3). We know from Genesis II, 9, that *the tree of life is in the midst of the garden*. Now just think for a moment: not only did this perfidious "God" set a trap for his creatures, but he deliberately caused a misunderstanding. For both of these trees were in the middle of the garden, and they were surely just alike. How could anyone know which was which? Esha in good faith had no idea of disobeying. Moreover (and here is another incongruity in imputing a fault to Esha), *she could not disobey* because the interdiction had been placed *only upon Adam.* Look at the situation again. Not only was there no prohibition laid upon Esha, but was not Esha herself created expressly so that Adam, in case he should eat of this fruit, would not "die a dead death" as would have been the case had he been left alone!

As to the creation of Adam and Esha, we hope you have admired the manner in which this deity complicated the operation. For him who had merely to speak the word to make the whole universe appear in the shortest possible time, why should it have been necessary, before creating man and woman, to reduce himself to human proportions? (Perhaps like Alice in Wonderland he drank of a bottle labelled "drink me" and became very small indeed.) He must have been no larger than human because otherwise he would not have been able to gather dust in order to make Adam, then blow into his nose, and later give him anaesthetics, extract a rib, go *walking in the garden in the cool of the day* (Gen. III, 8) and finally, in a true Victorian spirit of propriety, *make coats of skins* and clothe both man and woman (Gen. III, 21).

We shall not waste time on these puerilities. The attentive reader can find quite a number of them should he be so inclined. All we wish to emphasize is that serious-minded individuals, unable to accept certain parts of the text, simply pass over the most troublesome passages, placing them, in fact, outside the Revelation properly speaking. Such persons think they have shown broad-minded indulgence in overlooking numerous foolish details of ancient folklore which they regard as being due to the ignorance of copyists. But strangely enough, these very passages, re-read in their original letter-numbers, often reveal meanings which we can least afford to disregard. We have already said that it is not possible to reconcile the two readings, the familiar translation and the direct reading of the letter-numbers in the original Hebrew text. If we wish to read a text prepared for adults, we should abandon the mistranslations that have been current for so long.

Two questions arise: why is this story always read "upside down", and why does this version enjoy such great popularity? The answer springs from a profound psychological truth. The story, in its veritable nature, is frightening. But how can one be afraid of it if one has not understood it? The answer is that the psyche knows unconsciously that the story is dangerously upsetting. It creates a religious taboo to protect itself. The teaching that results from this translation is that mankind must remain in an infantile state and obey those who speak in the name of a "father" located in heaven. The dogma of original sin as disobedience is maintained to prevent disconcerting discoveries concerning that deity. For instance, an obvious ambiguity is created by YHWH with the two trees. Then, having created two adults who from the outset knew how to talk, why could not "he" or "it" have told them how to discriminate between a green and a red light (or how to recognize any other signal as being a danger zone, had there been one)? The truth is that this story is a magical snare where fear sees birth as sin, freedom as disobedience, nobleness as ruin. It is not the serpent who is the tempter. The deceiver is the so-called God, YHWH, and the deceived is the reader. Does this appear ridiculous? The scandal is the world-wide picture of a good old father seated in the heavens, benignly observing us.

If one reads the Bible correctly, one will see that the character of YHWH is always ambiguous. For instance, when Moses, who is afraid to go and meet Pharaoh, asks for advice in Midian (Exod. IV, 19), YHWH replies: *Go, return into Egypt: for all the men are dead which sought thy life.* This is equivalent to an ambush, for we are later told that *it came to pass by the way in the inn, that the Lord met him, and sought to kill him* (Exod. IV, 24). From the standpoint of this "God", Moses is a unique and invaluable collaborator. Without Moses, one may ask whether there would ever have been any Revelation at all. Then why should there be that treacherous move to lull Moses into a sense of false security, the better to assault him unawares? A man of weaker character and stamina, whose resistance was inadequate to the tasks that lay ahead, would have been killed. A deeper investigation into the matter reveals an aspect concerning the symbolic wife in whose house Moses came to rest. She had to undergo a test for maturity and awareness. Had she not been equal to the situation the human adventure undertaken by Moses would not have proceeded further.

Here is another example. It is in the story of Jacob's struggles against the angel. Long before Moses, Jacob is a most important figure in this ancient human history. We will discuss his story in detail later on. For the present, we read from the English translation of Genesis xxxix, 24-29 and find that *there wrestled a man with him* does not explain that the assailant is really Eesh, or YHWH. Jacob wrestles with him *until the break of day*. He clasps Eesh so closely that eventually Eesh cries out, *Let me go*; and he answers *I will not let thee go except thou bless me*. And when Eesh blesses him, he gives him his new name, Israel, signifying (according to the Hebrew as we read it): You have exerted your lordly power upon Elohim and Anashim (men as descendants), and you have consumed them. Eesh is no other than a personification of Elohim; and Israel knows very well what has happened, for he says: *I have seen Elohim face to face*.

Eesh, the archetype of Adam-Elohim is therefore none other than the total process of mankind.

The crux of the matter is this: whoever wrestles with Elohim and defeats him, is rewarded with his blessing; the blessing of course of life itself, and not of an absurd deity. In brief, Jacob, becoming Israel, reabsorbs the totality of duration, past and future. In many instances YHWH-Elohim appears thus as being life itself, unpredictable, unknowable, challenging. It remains for us to become alive to its intensity.

13

The Old Man of the Mothers

So FAR, we have expounded the significance of the Garden, the Trees, Adam, Esha and YHWH-Elohim. Only Nahhash, the serpent, remains to be studied, after which we will be in possession of all the clues concerning this allegory. The serpent plays an important part in many ancient myths. He appears in several cosmogonies as being present at the origin of creation, and at times as encompassing the earth. He has multiple meanings dealing with the general evolution of life, as well as with that of the individual in both body and psyche. In certain theosophies his name is *Kundalini*, and he springs from the genitals and ascends the spine. His "fire" is initiatory and becomes knowledge through transmutation of sex into creative intelligence. Factually, the serpent is phallic and nakedly so. (Genesis III, 1 ought not to read, *now the serpent was more subtle than any beast*, but "more naked".)

Hidden and coiled inside hollows and cavities of the earth, he suddenly darts out with swift swinging blows. He is therefore considered mythically as being the son of Earth, the male energy born into the primordial Mothers. Is he not that Phallus, the very resurrection of *Aleph* from its earthly entombment? Is he not the best possible resurrection of *Aleph*, according to Eretz's capacity at the time?

Somewhere in the background of our ancestral memory we have a fossilized stratum recalling that the earth put forth great and successive efforts in order to engender beings that could stand upright. The biblical serpent who appears upright is the symbolic descendant of the great saurians of early geological epochs, creatures that occupied the planet for millions of years prior to man's appearance. This serpent is then the symbol of the most alive creature that earth was able to produce until a certain epoch.

Now there are Adam and Esha, symbolizing an absolutely new era. Who are they: she the spouse of fire (or the feminine fire), he no longer knowing whether he is Adam or Eesh? It is as if they were not wholly there, as if they were just emerging from oblivion. Adam, especially, is almost entirely asleep. Does he not resemble a newborn child? While the animal species respond to life with a series of automatic reflexes suited to their needs, this Adam will have to learn about everything without recourse to animal instinct. Just here at the extreme limit of a passing era appears the old, the very old serpent who originally symbolized the "male" begotten by Adamah.

Nahhash, the carrier of all the memories of time, of all forgotten wisdom, now has the mission of transmitting duration to these two new beings; for until they possess the totality of time, they will not be wholly incarnate. They cannot exist unless this last link is provided. They must consume the past and be its fruition. Within them, as they are presented in this story, there already exists the intermittent pulsation of life-death—life-death. They must become the whole game of life, not only this discontinuous element but the continuous as well. The mission of Nahhash, the serpent, is to plunge them into what one can, in a sense, call evolution. He must transmit his life to them; he must join the "earth" fire to their fire from "heaven".

He cannot transmit this to Adam who is as unstable as if he had been knocked on the head. But the serpent tentatively addresses Esha: "Has Elohim really said: You shall not eat of every tree?" The answer should have been: "No, it was YHWH-Elohim, not Elohim, who said some such thing—not to me, but to Adam. And he said it because at that time Adam was alone and if he had eaten of that tree, he would not have survived a single instant. That is why YHWH-Elohim created me—so that Adam could eat of that tree without dying." Had Esha thus responded with the true facts, this story would never have become so widely accepted as it is. Why? If we are not afraid, we can find the answer to that question.

14

Are We Afraid of the Bible?

WE WANT the psychological security of a protecting deity, whereas we can become *as gods, knowing good and evil* (Gen. III, 5), just as the serpent said. This statement, which really means that we can be the whole process "Elohim", is confirmed by YHWH-Elohim: *the man is become as one of us* (Gen. III, 22). Rabbi Yhshwh, better known as Jesus, is supposed to have quoted that assertion; but, of course, he who referred to himself as Ben-Adam (mistranslated as "Son of man") knew the meaning of the letter-numbers. Not even his disciples understood that sacred language, as they themselves said. This understanding is not easy, but it is one thing to make a serious attempt to understand a somewhat difficult code, and it is quite another to run away from it and to dream that the mystery of life-death and existence can reveal itself by means of a few legends.

The fact (which one can verify for oneself) is that the copyists, priests, rabbis and theologians have systematically discarded every statement in the Bible that destroys man's sense of security in a steady continuity of existence. But the Bible is a Revelation only in so far as it includes death in life, thereby disrupting every psychological certainty. Vested authority throughout the ages, however, has reversed and betrayed this biblical message of life-including-death and has promised existence-after-death, which is not the same thing at all. Death is actually here, as a vital aspect of our everyday life, at every moment. When we come to see that we are constantly waging a battle (psychologically) for the continuity of our existence against the life-death within us, and when we come to learn (from the Book of Genesis) that that combat must cease by our becoming that very life-death, a disruption occurs in our thought process and in our psychical armour, which liberates us into life. And this is precisely the thing, the life-stimulating thing, that we are afraid of.

It is important to learn that our urge towards static permanence goes very deep. Constantly, we shy away from something that might upset us. This we automatically classify as "harmful". For instance, look again at the tree which, so the translations state, is "the tree of knowledge of good and evil". The schema *Tov*, translated "good", expresses the static, materializing, carnal action of the primitive female (symbolically considered under all its aspects). That action nourishes and strengthens the *Bayt*, the "house", the shell.

The schema *Raa* ("evil") leads all structured energy towards the indetermination of 70; it cannot therefore but tend to destroy all that is static, determinant, conditioning.

Any static factor in our minds eventually jeopardizes the flow of newness, of freshness, which is the specific quality of human genesis. The cause of fear is easy to see: one does not want to be disturbed; therefore one calls good anything which is the mind's container, and calls evil everything which will endanger the maintenance of one's armour of certainties. And the translators, by supporting this reversal, have seen to it that we should be conditioned to a view of life that mocks all true values. When one reflects that *Tov* (translated "good") really means limited in its material proliferation and that the process *Raa* (translated "evil") is really a loosening of our bonds, a thawing out, an awakening or quickening of the life force, one can understand that the action of *Raa*, far from being in any sense evil, is something designed to save our life.

The misunderstandings with which we have grown up are too numerous to be dealt with in one small volume. Here, however, is another vital example. We have seen with the episode of Jacob wrestling with Elohim that the process of evolution in time is satisfied only when overcome and "conquered". Thus Esha, in plucking the apple, understands and integrates the

Elohimic process and it is satisfied. An extraordinary thing then happens to Esha. When she is questioned concerning this event, she does not—as the translations assert—reply, *The serpent beguiled me* (Gen. III, 13). What the true reading gives is far more significant. The Hebrew phrase, *Hanahhash Hashayiny*, as is so often true in the most beautiful passages, is impossible to translate in two or three words. It has to do with the action of the letter *Sheen* which we met with after Adam's so-called sleep. *Sheen* (300), it is remembered, stands for the cosmic breath of life, and we have seen that the true meaning is not that they were "naked" and "not-ashamed" (which has nothing to do with the letter-numbers of the text), but that they were left without the *Sheen*. Now *Hanahhash Hashayiny* simply means that Nahhash, the serpent, "*Sheens*" her: that is, he blends his earthly fire with her lost heavenly fire, which thus comes to life again. Some traditions have identified this *Sheen* (300) with the mythical "Spirit of God".

But we are afraid to pluck the fruit; and because we wish to rationalize our "sins" of omission, we invent a prohibition and carefully project the allegory into the past, when in fact the fruit is ready for us to harvest here and now. Esha did not live centuries ago, and we wonder if she is even born yet.

The psychological process by which a revelatory and pro-foundly challenging book is consistently and forever misread is, after all, quite easy to understand. The reason that the tale of the talking serpent and the magic apple outlives every other fairy story is that we are afraid of it.

15

A General View of the Issues Involved

ESHA, STIRRED by the whirl of life transmitted to her by the serpent, awakens. The fruit she has eaten develops her sensorial faculties, as well as those of Adam. This is the birth of *Homo sapiens*. Psychic energy (what the psychologists call libido) invades her body. The sexual urge is dominated and sublimated through a new sensibility. This sensibility is generated in Esha by the eating of a fresh and perfect fruit, the life of which antedates all animal evolution. This life is transmuted directly into Esha, without the least connection with the intervening phases of evolution, represented by the serpent.

The dialogues between YHWH-Elohim, Adam, Esha and Nahhash must be read from the original letter-numbers in order to savour their real meaning to the full. The familiar words and phrases, "afraid", "naked", "I hid myself", "woman", "beguiled", "cursed", "enmity between serpent and woman", "in sorrow thou shall bring forth children", "cursed is the ground for thy sake", "dust thou art", etc., are all corruptions. We cannot read chapter titles in the English Bible, such as *The serpent deceives Eve* or *The punishment of mankind*, without feeling—as we see the incredible results of fear—a surge of both anger and compassion. It blocks even one's capacity to read. Eve does not even exist at this point in Eden. Esha is not Eve: Hhevah, who is Eve, comes later (Gen. III, 20). And for God's sake (or for man's) why should the earth be cursed? The neurotic idea that a divinity can curse is crude, primitive, prehistoric. This idea of a curse is born out of fear. Can "God" be afraid?

Misinterpreted for centuries, the Bible has been a fatal cancer in the mind. Its vitalizing beauty still awaits discovery. The symbolic ejection of Adam from the womb (called Eden) is an allegory of a birth. Do you see that to call this birth a curse is to refuse it? Do you see that ideas of punishment and a fall based upon this false premise retard the genesis of all human beings? And what happens if a birth is unduly delayed? The foetus dies.

The end of Genesis, chapter III, 24 by comparison with the original text seen through its letter-numbers, is madness. If our deity is Life, why did "he" place *at the east of the garden of Eden the Cherubim, and a flaming sword which turned every way to keep the way of the tree of life?* Can Life put an obstacle to life? Unless we understand that—psychically—the angel has to be assaulted, overcome and literally consumed and that the flaming sword and even the tree of life itself have to be eaten up, digested and absorbed, we shall continue to cling to the miserable, cramped and frightened existence we call life; and the fear of "evil" (good) and "death" (life) by which we deceive ourselves into projecting the so-called religious standards of morality will ensure our continued exploitation.

Before we proceed into Genesis IV, where all the personages are archetypes, let us recapitulate the contents of Genesis I, II and III, as read from their letter-numbers.

Genesis I: The anatomy of the process of intermittent energy "associated-against" a continuum of space-time. The interiorization of that energy within the continuum. The continuum becomes autonomous.

Genesis II: Consequences of the autonomy of the continuum (self-induction). This process as seen from the interior. The appearance of YHWH and of the germ in which unconditioned energy can and must rise again. Neither life in its character of discontinuous, pulsating, immeasurable energy nor life in its character of the continuum-existence would be anything, one without the other; nor could either even exist if they were not playing each against the other.

Genesis III: The anatomy of the human germ in which this interplay between existence and life takes place. The incarnation of this germ. In man is centrifugal energy, buried, dormant in his very blood. This energy only expresses itself by unco, ordinated outbursts of activity. The real issue—the resurrection of organic, creative energy—depends upon woman; the female in her, being by nature the protectress of the continuum, existence, must transform itself. Esha takes the decisive step and brings about a transformation of the animal erotic-sensorial faculties; the eating of the fruit is an allegorical representation of the blending of existence and life within the human kind of the two players.

As we shall see, Genesis iv deals with the implanting of this whole process in the human psyche by means of personifications of the cosmic interplay of energy and mass, both within and without ourselves.

16

Genesis IV: The Archetypes

ADAM HAS now emerged from the womb, but he remains until Genesis x (Noah's posterity) a mythical, symbolic being. He is still merely a legend and rightly so. He is, as yet, far too immature for his presence to be felt in the world of existence. In simple terms, Adam expelled from Eden means that this myth declares mankind to be born. The text says that only Adam is expelled, not *Esha*. When Adam names his wife *Hheva* he extracts her from the archetype *Esha*. We must not forget that in the Bible a new name given to a person indicates a mutation. *Esha*, abstract schema, spouse of the cosmic fire, remains inside Eden, whereas a different personification, Hheva, accompanies Adam in his earthly adventure.

But in this embryology a (declared) birth is a fixation in a pre-human state. Therefore historical man must constantly revise his notions of what is really human, whilst historical woman must unfold the inner *Hheva*, symbol of accomplished womanhood, of transcendent femininity, that has yet to come into being.

Since she appears at the beginning of this phase of the story, she must be understood. From the outset, she represents in womanhood everything which, much later on, Yhshwh (known as Jesus) represents in manhood. This is evident from her letter-numbers *Hhayt-Waw-Hay*, which are a projection of YHWH. If it is understood that Hheva thus embodies in her very nature the supreme archetype of womanhood, it will be seen that there is no need to deify any woman, virgin or otherwise. Hheva being a materialized counterpart of YHWH, this archetype is shown to be at the very core of life-in-existence

Esha, still in the womb of Eden, is the inexhaustible flame, always alive. Hheva is that flame in existence: the complete archetype. In fact, all the personages in Genesis IV are archetypes.

The human psyche—yours and that of everyone born since the appearance of *Homo sapiens*—is enclosed within itself, much as if it were a chrysalis enclosed within its self-spun cocoon. Or again, human consciousness encased in the ego, is similar to a traveller who has taken shelter from imminent danger in a securely locked cabin. In the midst of the surrounding human and cosmic violence, the voices of initiates—those who have perceived the essentials—describe the interplay of existence and of the non-temporal. But the projections of the archetypes here involved (Adam, Eve, Cain, Abel, etc.) strike the protective shell of the psyche and cause reactions that distort it and are often the very opposite of what the archetypes represent. The psyches enclosed in their cells of refuge perceive in the message of the archetypes nothing but the voice of the big bad wolf who, so they think, is trying to demolish their dwellings, their *Bayt*—as in fact he is, though with motives they cannot evaluate.

But these archetypes, personifying as they do the cosmic interplay of energy and mass, inner as well as outer, are the framework upon which our psyches build themselves. The archetypes, Adam (static) and Eve (dynamic), are in us prior even to the formation of our psyches. Whatever their names, they exist in every human being. In some parts of the world they may be called Vishnu and Shiva, or Yin and Yang, or otherwise. Since the constant reaction of the psyches is that of self-protection, these archetypes are perceived as being positive when they are negative, and static when in fact they are dynamic. Though we may glimpse traces of reality within the essence of our nature we cannot fathom this essence as long as, in the interplay between life and existence, we identify ourselves with existence, duration, and a past which we project into the future.

In other words, we are forever placing ourselves in opposition to, and in conflict with, the vital action of the archetypes, at the very origin of our psyches; and in so doing, we continually propel ourselves into a contradiction that becomes more and more intense. We are the containing elements of the archetypes, as well as the resistance to what they contain. We are at the same time life and that which encompasses life, providing the resistance enabling life to manifest itself. Whenever this resistance becomes too strong, the life force cannot get through to us.

We see the approach of this phenomenon when we become obsessed with the acquisition of multitudes of "things"—automobiles, television sets, gadgets of all sorts, enormous bank accounts, etc.—and when we begin to consider such things as being indispensable to life. When these or other materialistic and mechanistic pursuits absorb our attention and energies, we are headed for a salutary, though drastic and at times painful lesson. Sometimes such a crisis—particularly where we fail to comprehend its significance—can be deadly in its effect.

We have already mentioned the destruction of Jerusalem, its people, its temples and palaces by YHWH. It is only one example of the persistent destruction of "containers" by life-death.

It is essential for us to understand that if we, existence-in-life, are contemptuously oblivious of the livingness in which we have our being, then life-in-existence reasserts itself in no uncertain terms. In our daily living we are seldom aware of being in the grip of these complementary forces, but they are everywhere discernible once our eyes are opened. Our world of today is perilously unbalanced, reflecting our inner states of chronic disorder. Either we execute an about-face within our psyche or we drift into stagnant waters, or worse. We must change places in the game and so liberate the quality of life which Nahhash, the serpent, brought forth in Hheva.

Returning to Genesis IV, 1, and the birth of Qaheen* (not to be pronounced Cain), we see that after he is born Hhevah says, *Qaneetee* Eesh Et *YHWH*, which does not at all mean: *I have begotten a man with the aid of the Lord.*

We have already stated that the schema *Et* (*Aleph-Tav*) is a combination of the first and last letters and corresponds to our expression "from A to Z". The translators have totally neglected it in the first verse of Genesis (the creation of *Et Ha-Shamaim* and *Et Ha-Eretz*). This *Et*, every time that it is used, indicates that the schemata referred to are equations in the form of blunt formulas which include (from A to Z) the premisses and the conclusions of given processes. They are, therefore, if we understand their unfoldment, both the summing up of the problems and their solutions.

So when Hheva says: I have "acquired" (we can keep that translation for the time being) *Eesh Et YHWH*, she actually says that she has "acquired" the archetype *Eesh* which "from A to Z" *is YHWH*.

The consecrated version: "I have acquired a man from the Lord" is an unforgivable betrayal of the text. It weighed and still weighs heavily upon the minds of millions. Its responsibility in our human misfortunes is beyond evaluation.

We begin here to understand why, according to Qabala, the archetype *Hheva* is so important. It is the first time that YHWH is mentioned alone, without Elohim, and it is mentioned by the woman *Hheva*, in a flash that pierces through the entire process of duration.

Considering the exceptional importance of that passage and the historically disastrous interpretations concerning *Qaheen*, we must briefly analyse the schema *Qaneetee* (*Qof-Noun-Yod-Tav-Yod*: 100.50.10.400.10). It includes the very name of Qaheen (Cain) with the permutation of *Noun-Yod* instead of *Yod-Noun*, so arranged as to block 400 in between two *Yod*. Those two *Yod* are the sign of a double existence and can be interpreted as

* The use of "Q" for the "K" sound is unavoidable, since Q (100) and K (20) are not interchangeable, meaning-wise.

expressing the objective and the subjective spheres. The 400 is the resistance (as of a chalice) of the Creation to the cosmic *Aleph* (*Qof*:100) that is in it (and yet overflowing).

It is not by mere chance that the schemata *Qaneetee* and *Qaheen* begin with the *Qof* of Qabala.

When eventually Hheva gives birth to Hevel (not to be pronounced Abel), it is not even said that Adam "knew his wife again". But later on, after the disappearance of Hevel, it *is* said: *And Adam knew his wife again: and she bore a son, and called his name Seth: For God, said she, hath appointed me another seed instead of Abel, whom Cain slew* (Gen. IV, 25). Here we must read Elohim for God, Hevel for Abel, and Qaheen for Cain; thus the final phrase becomes: Hevel whom Qaheen has shattered. We will presently explain the difference between the "shattering" and the "slaying" of the traditional version.

For the moment, notice the difference between these three births: (*a*) In the case of Qaheen, Hheva entirely overlooks the role of Adam; this corresponds to the obliteration of Joseph, spouse of Mary, by the Church. Hheva declares and affirms: I have acquired Eesh, the living cosmic fire, which is YHWH (the process of life-in-existence). In other words, she is defining the terminal omega of the allegory: the resurrection through womanhood of the immeasurable energy incarnate in existence. No passage in Genesis is clearer than this, or as total and absolute. The ending of the allegory is fully implied in its beginning. Qaheen is YHWH incarnate. Any other interpretation is psychological murder. (*b*) Hevel is nothing more than the carnal proliferation of the female in Hheva. This son has nothing of Adam, or rather he has from Adam solely the *dam* (blood in Hebrew: the blood which Adamah drinks). (*c*) With the birth of Set, who takes the place of Hevel, Hheva recognizes that it is Elohim who is there. Elohim, it will be recalled, is the evolutionary process within the duration of existence. It is this Set who will become the mythical ancestor of the human race.

It cannot be overemphasized that the ecclesiastical tradi-

135

tions, giving as they do the words "God" for Elohim and "the Lord" for YHWH, bar the road to the understanding of the Bible. It is important to remember the real significance of these two schemas at the outset of any study concerning Qaheen. Elohim (*Aleph-Lammed-Hay-Yod-Mem*), read according to code (1.30.5.10.40), expresses the fact that the timeless discontinuous pulsation which is *Aleph* (1) underlies the functional movement of organisms (30), their life (5), and all existence (10) with their resistance to life (40). Thus Elohim is both an unique and a plural process. This process of life-death-in-existence is the only active agent in Genesis I. It can only put into motion the repetitive production of prototypes, until the "blessing" and "sanctifying" of no. 7 in Genesis II, 3, which opens the way to all indeterminate possibilities.

YHWH is an altogether different sphere of life. Its schema 10.5.6.5 can only be actualized when the copulation (6) really takes place between 5 and 5, and that can only happen in mankind, between body and psyche. Obviously it cannot happen between a nutshell and its nut, nor between an eggshell and its germ, and no animal can ever decide to take control over its own body.

The key to this we already know: it resides in the mutually fertile relationship—5.6.5—of the two aspects of life with which we have been dealing all along: the existence and the immanence, the temporal and the timeless, the finite and the transcendent, the outer and the inner, the container and the contained, the objective and the subjective, etc. All this, of course, has nothing to do with any "lord" or "God" to be worshipped. It has to do with a relationship of inter-fertilization that can happen at the moment of our "seeing" it. And we can only see it when we strip off our Abel skin and understand and become Cain, fully alive and responsive.

★

The allegory of Qaheen, though short, is so full of detail that we can only give the essentials of it. Does Qaheen—a bit stunned in the capacity of YHWH incarnate—"till the ground"? No. He establishes his dominion over Adamah (see letter-numbers). And Hevel establishes his dominion over the flesh of the herds. In the process of time (after the passing of an era) Qaheen establishes a relationship between YHWH and himself. Hevel then imitates him and produces offerings to YHWH. There is nothing wrong with Hevel; since he cannot help being a specimen of ordinary, petty, toiling humanity. YHWH accepts his offerings. But Qaheen, being YHWH itself, incarnate but in a state of amnesia, worships an image of himself, which he projects, thereby creating a distance between himself and himself. Since this form of worship reflects a lack of self-knowledge, it is rejected.

This drama is at the core of human experience. We are told that Christ is within, or that there is an Atman, immortal soul or essence within us. Instead of plunging into that living life, what do we do? We worship a picture of what we suppose it is, which cannot be but a projection of its shell or container.

The dialogue which results from these rejected offerings, if correctly read, is one of great beauty. In fact, it is a soliloquy within YHWH the archetype and YHWH incarnate. The few verses which follow (until Genesis IV, 16) are one of the summits of the archives of humanity. If we enter into this soliloquy, if it comes alive in our hearts and minds, we penetrate into all the suffering in the world; the suffering of love, of death. And beyond and above it, incorruptible life can come into being.

We must allow our mind to be still, then ask ourselves sincerely whether we can make head or tail of the following little speech: *If thou doest well, shalt thou not be accepted? and if thou doest not well, sin lieth at the door. And unto thee shall be his desire, and thou shalt rule over him* (Gen. IV, 7). Somehow Qaheen comes to understand the riddle in the original form of the verse—which (fortunately for him) is not expressed in the existing translation. YHWH has no need to explain it. Its key, hidden in its letter-numbers, can be discovered and lived in freedom. It is the key

137

of life. Were it a teaching or a commandment, Qaheen would obey it, thereby losing his and his brother's freedom by becoming his "brother's keeper".

The Hebrew text of this verse, when read in current language, is not correct grammatically. It mixes the masculine and feminine of certain words. But there is no logic in judging a text according to the grammatical rules of a different language. We must therefore discover whether the apparent mistakes make sense when we read them, according to the code, as they are.

The text begins with a schema which is approximately read "Hello". It is not translated in the English version, and in some other versions it is supposed to be an interjection meaning more or less "Isn't it?". Its letter-numbers are *Hay-Lammed-Vav-Aleph*: 5.30.6.1; and as is the case in several other important verses we are here dealing with an "opening statement" in the form of an equation which this verse is meant to solve. When 5.30.6.1. is solved in action within us, the revelation is there; Qaheen will understand it and act accordingly. His mission— mythically, that of God in exile—is to give life (5), organic movement (30) and fertility (6) to Aleph (1).

The following schema is *Aleph-Mem—Tav-Yod-Tayt-Yod-Vayt*: 1.40—400.10.9.10.2. It describes what happens when *Aleph* cannot overcome the resistance of *Mem* (40): it becomes buried in cosmic resistance (400) in which the original female archetype (9) is solidly encased in between two *Yod* (10.9.10) for the benefit of its personal dwelling (2). This schema is read *Teeteev*, which, as a word in the ordinary language, is derived from *Tov* and means "Thou doest well". This unfortunate "doing well" leads to the following schema, *Sh-et*: 300.1000.400, in which we witness the cosmic organic life (300) of the most exalted *Aleph* (1000) desperately hurling itself against the obstinate resistance of 400. The ecclesiastical interpretation, has it thus: "Shalt thou not be accepted?"

Such is the alternative for *Aleph*. From then on the schemata, till the end of the verse, are an analysis of the other alternative, Aleph's resurrection and its action upon any individual. It begins by negating the Teeteev thus: *Vayim Lo Teeteev* and *Vayim Lo* is: 6.1000.600—30.1000. Some texts emphasize the cosmic nature of these numbers, *Aleph* as 1000 and *Mem* as 600, by enlarging them graphically (as an echo of the original code?). This considerable reinforcement of *Aleph* and *Mem* makes a tremendous impact on *Teeteev* and upsets it.

We thus see in the next schema an organic movement (30) grafted, so to speak, on the undifferentiated reservoir of life (80) and the cosmic resistances—existence yielding to this life as archetype (8). This schema, therefore, is 30.80.400.8. It is pronounced, as a word, *Lepetahh* and is meant to be, in its translations, "at the door". However, even in colloquial Hebrew, *Petahh* (or *Fetahh*) is meant to be any opening. We have here, an example of the debasing of the ontological language into a sensorial, image-making idiom. The opening truly exists: it is in the organic motion (30) granted to the primal life, non-identified, non-evolved, from which the original female draws its life.

We now come upon the drama which is so often described symbolically in the Book of Genesis: the reaction of the female. The following schema is *Hhatat*: 8.9.1.400. The sequence is obvious; let us look at it again: 30.80.400.8—8.9.1.400. We see that the action upon 80 and 8 was aiming at the female (9). And now, in spite of the 400 still waging a rear-guard defence, *Aleph* has been introduced in close contact to 9 (this action expressed by 8.9.1.400 is strangely enough translated "sin").

The result of this penetration is an inner turmoil in the female (or the unconscious, in the psyche); and this new vibration is an extraordinary peace and flowering, a cosmic transfiguration of the feminine, a dialogue being born between the deep layers of the unconscious and the outer consciousness.

This flowering is expressed in the schema which follows: *Robetz* (*Raysh-Bayt-Tsadde*: 200.2.900). Now the "house" (2) is cognizant of its cosmic appurtenance (200), and the feminine is totally transfigured (900). As often happens in current Hebrew, this schema, read as a word (*Robetz*) has two con-

139

trasting meanings: to lie down and brood, and to sprinkle or spread knowledge, Ontologically, both meanings are correct and not at all contradictory.

We now come to the schema which, in Hebrew and in every translation, is supposed to mean "and unto thee": *Weyilekh* (6.1.30.10.500). It expresses the productive (6) drive of *Aleph* (1) imparting functional movement (30) to its eternal "partner-against" (10). Here they at last meet and the result is 500: cosmic life in existence!

The following schema depicts the game, the interplay which results from this happy meeting. It is read, more or less, *Teshooq-too*. The root *Shooq* is the oriental bazaar, where all goods are exchanged. The schema is 400.300.6.100.400.6. We see the 6 in it twice, one being in between two 400s and one outside. This schema opens an infinite vista to our meditation. It shows, in action, the cosmic "breath" (300) constantly in fertile symbiosis with the cosmic *Aleph*, happily alive in the cosmos. The final 6 leads us in the spirit of hope to the last three schemata, the concluding two being linked with a hyphen *Ve-ata Timshal-Bo*: 6.1.400.5—400.40.300.30—2.6. This conclusion of verse 7 (note this number again) of chapter IV (note this number, too), opens an inexhaustible field for meditation and knowledge: the drastic cleavage between 400.40 and 300.30.

In résumé, we have learned from this verse that if and when the cosmic *Aleph* is alive and active in us, it permeates directly the unconscious and silences it, after which an exalted, scintillating stillness permeates our being in fruitful commerce and consummation, beyond time and beyond evolution. The inner dialogue is instantaneous in its effect. Qaheen understands its message. He becomes the container of timeless life; and, as such, he goes toward Hevel—man conditioned according to his time and location—and speaks to him, although their separation has already taken place. But Hevel cannot understand; he cannot even hear Qaheen's parable, and he dissolves into what he essentially is: a bladder of blood. This blood is drunk by the female, Earth. The text does not say that Qaheen slays Hevel:

it says that he *is Yaqam*, meaning elevated, raised, exalted above Hevel.

So YHWH and Qaheen look for Hevel and do not find him. There is only that pool of blood which Adamah, the enormous female-to-be-conquered, is drinking. And it is the curse of this female which is upon Qaheen. It is preposterous to think that he is cursed by "God". On the contrary, it is written: *Therefore whosoever slayeth Cain, vengeance (of YHWH) shall be taken on him sevenfold* (Gen. IV, 15). Qaheen will always re-emerge seven times more strongly: his number is 7: *Qof-Yod-Noun* terminal (100.10.700). It is an intense life, terrifying to whoever curses it. Qaheen, as life-death, life-death, is the ceaseless, intermittent pulsation that will always triumph over the female element of resistance forged with blood. He is here, now, present, as he was present always, although more often than not unidentified.

All this is, as well as it can be put, the literal meaning of the Scriptures. The historical reaction to it is the sanguinary, cruel and frightful history of man throughout the ages. In these thousands of years, more and more worse and worse wars have succeeded one another. We have wholesale murder, racial hatred, hatred between peoples of different coloured skins, different nationalities, different religious or economic creeds— each individual killing in order to "protect" himself (as if in killing, one were not killing oneself) whilst Cain is "righteously" disgraced and ostracized.

During all this time, while "Cain" (misinterpreted) is forever cursed by mankind's unending fratricide, Qaheen, who cannot prevent Hevel being killed by his own conditioning, is in deepest mourning *in the land of Nod* (Nod means sorrow.) This land is *east of Eden*, there where the tree of life is. This "land of Nod" is none other than the Land of *Yod*, where the Y is brought to life in N (50): *Noun-Vav-Dallet* instead *Yod-Vav-Dallet*.

The verse (Gen. IV, 16) dealing with Qaheen's "going out from the presence of the Lord" describes an action concerning Qaheen in relation to an aspect (or projection) of YHWH in the world of time and evolution where Qaheen must live—or, to put it differently, where YHWH must become incarnate. The verse begins thus: *Veyotse Qaheen Melafne YHWH.* The action *Veyotse* (6.10.90.1) states the equation that the verse must solve: Qaheen's mission will be to apply fecundity (6) to the existence of Yod (10) so to elevate the female to its power (90) and thus liberate *Aleph* (1). He will do it *Melafne YHWH*— which, in numbers is 40.30.80.50.10—YHWH. We see that every one of these numbers is a multiple of 10, i.e. existential. Through 40, the 30 acts upon 80 and the 50 upon 10. This signifies that in (or by) the resistance of existence (40) the movement (organic) of 30 is given to the reservoir of primordial existence (80) and that life-in-existence (50) is given to Yod (10). This action is, in a nutshell, the definition of YHWH (10.5.6.5). One of the fives of YHWH acts as 30 upon 80, the other as 50 upon 10. Thus are interpreted the two lives with which we have been concerned all along, the 30 affecting the contained (germ of life-to-be), the 50 its container (*Yod*).

The last two schemata of this verse, *Qedmat-Eden*, translated "east of Eden", are: 100.4.40.400—70.4.700. They are like a thunderbolt, a fantastic *coup de théâtre*, for anyone who would doubt the meaning of this code. They show *Qof* acting as a spear and piercing through and through every layer of resistance (4.40.400), every crystallization of the mind, every established certainty, and projecting the archetype (4) of such resistance into the actualization of all possible possibilities (70) and its cosmic significance (700). This action, this preservation of every possibility, obviously destroys every prototype, everything which is fixed, established, or built to endure.

It is not surprising that for the conditioned mind Cain is a killer, whereas he is the very action of YHWH.

17

Intermezzo

GENESIS IV, 17-26 is very interesting, but we are afraid it would confuse the issue were we to go into it even briefly. The same holds true of Genesis V, in spite of its great importance. This chapter deals with the two lines of descent that originated with Adam. The first line, by YHWH, is continued through Qaheen. The other, by Elohim, is transmitted by way of Set.

Both of these descents are, of course, purely symbolic. They are however, intimately interrelated since that of Qaheen constantly reacts upon the pseudo-historical descent of Set.

We are dealing here with an astonishing poem in code, respecting that interplay of cosmic energies which has, from the very beginning, been the constant subject-matter of the Book of Genesis: the immanent energy of Qaheen is projected from the interior, or the "inner light", and is in no way subject to time. That of Set is concerned with the evolution of the "containers" and with their special and particular forms or shapes. As we have already learned, the ultimate purpose of this interplay is Indetermination.

In Genesis IV and V every name has a meaning: Enoch and Enos, Mehujael and Mahalalel, etc, as well as the phrases introducing each name, whether it is or is not said that so and so "lived and begat", whether their days are eight hundred and ninety-five or only sixty-five, whether Lamekh takes two wives and avenges Qaheen seventy and sevenfold, or whether Enoch "walks with God", or whether there is a relation between the seven generations through Qaheen and the ten through Set. All this calls for a rather complicated analysis of the relationship between numerous archetypes and historical humanity. It

143

clearly shows the significance of Qaheen and his action upon the generations of Set. Meaningful as these interrelationships are, for the time being their further development must be put aside, because of their great number and complexity. Were we to attempt a transcription coupled with constant explanations of the code we would soon be lost in a maze. That chapter must be read directly with full knowledge of the graphs and code.

Likewise, we will not go at length into the story of the Deluge, although the origins of this legend reveal certain elements of the conflict between the different symbols which we have been examining. The incoherence in the behaviour of a divinity who decides to suppress all life because his creation has gone sour, and who in this drastic operation carefully preserves a sample of each of his created species so that he can keep alive what he intends to destroy, is a stepping-down to the folklore level of some of the contradictions with which we are now familiar. And the picturesque Odyssey of Noahh and his Ark furnishes amusing decorations for nurseries.

The Deluge, no doubt, was really a cataclysm that was apparently the end of a world and, for those to whom it happened, the end of *the* world. Then came the surprising discovery that everything was beginning again. The Semitic genius grafted some interesting symbols onto these archaic memories, such as the Ark itself, the raven, the dove, and of course, all the numbers involved: one hundred and fifty days of water, the grounding of the Ark on the seventeenth day in the seventh month, the decreasing of the waters until the tenth month, the name Ararat, etc. Each episode of this legend merits careful study, but we shall keep to its broad lines.

After the Deluge, we leave the archetypes and enter into another domain. Here the archetypes, the framework on which the psyche builds itself, engender categories of symbols. One can follow these until the fiftieth and last chapter of Genesis which concludes with Joseph's death at the symbolic age of a hundred and ten years. Then one can trace the development of these symbols right through into the Gospels of Matthew and John.

We have already shown the keys to the understanding of these stories. The general tenor of them is as follows: the principal themes are the allegories of (a) *Aleph* in the blood and *Aleph*'s inevitable resurrection; (b) the earth (soil) as Adamah— the female of Adam—and Adam as being mankind; (c) Elohim seen as the life-process of *Aleph* and *Aleph* as pulsating discontinuity life-death, Elohim being its movement and its projection into the continuity of existence; (d) the story of Esha and Eesh, being archetypes of "fiery" womanhood and manhood; (e) the nature of YHWH as being the double life (inner and outer) of all lives which can only come into being in mankind where the two lives fertilize each other; (f) the interplay between life and existence (life as life-death—life-death operating upon the existence of all that exists); (g) the perpetual delaying of the birth of the human germ, always prevented from settling down into any fixed or permanent conditioning as is the case for the germs of life in the animal kingdom; (h) the wrestling between Elohim and YHWH; (i) the conflict between YHWH and Adamah, hence the conflict of their so-called "sons"—in other words, between the offspring of YHWH through Adam and the offspring of the Mothers (Adamah); (j) finally, and most important to full understanding, the process of womanhood's sublimation.

In spite of their seeming complexity, were they alive within us through one single act of understanding, all these themes would sow the seed of Revelation in our being. Let us now pass on to a consideration of some of the major landmarks which high-point the extraordinary unity in the line of thought which acts upon us, from the myth of Adam to the myth of Jesus.

18

Noahh and his Sons

GENESIS IX, 5. Here is another unfortunate example of the inadequacy of the translations. After blessing Noahh and giving him instructions, "God" says to him: *And surely the blood of your lives will I require; at the hand of every beast will I require it, and at the hand of man; at the hand of every man's brother will I require the life of man.*

We submit that this makes no sense at all. In its correct reading, this verse refers to the conflict between YHWH and Adamah, who disputes the blood of Adam. YHWH does not "require" it (Noah's, i.e. Adam's, blood); the letter-numbers state, rather, that he confers upon it a cosmic significance and the cosmic energy of *Sheen.*

It is surprising that among the different meanings of the root Hhai the one selected by the translators is "beast". We know that when leaving Eden Adam *called the name of his wife Hheva because she was the mother of Kol Hhai*: "all living" (Gen. III, 20). The conflict between *YHWH* and *Adamah* is now taken over by the evolutionary process *Elohim-Noahh.*

You remember that Adamah (earth), "opening her mouth", drank Hevel's *dam* (blood), poor Hevel being no more than that. The *dam* of Adam must sublimate itself—the *Mem* of its name must jump from its lower value 40 to its exalted value 600, and the letter-numbers explain that Adam must become the "brother" of Eesh; we now understand that this mutation is to be brought about through blending man as a product of the earth with man endowed with celestial fire.

Genesis IX, *13.* The appearance of the rainbow as a covenant is, of course, a resurrection of light (*Awr,* whose letters are

146

Aleph-Waw-Raysh) above the "waters" (the carriers of life).

Genesis IX, *20.* Noahh becomes a "husbandman" and plants a vineyard, say the English translators. It is interesting to note that the word husbandman for farmer is literally correct. Noahh transmutes downwards his "Eesh" quality of fire by becoming Eesh (husband) to Adamah (the earth). The earth reproduces this fire as wine (the wine as symbol expresses that fact, as the Qabala well knows).

Genesis IX, *21.* The strange fruit of the nuptials between Eesh (as man-fire) and Adamah is Yeen (*Yod-Yod-Noun*) a double existence in number 700. (Notice that 700 is also the key-number to Qaheen.) This *Yeen* is a sort of tornado in which anything can happen. The English word wine is the Hebrew word scarcely modified; so also is the Latin. (Incidentally, it is not generally realized how many of our words derive from, or are, the Hebrew ones.)

This verse exemplifies the fact that the symbols of blood and wine belong to the same category. Having drunk, Noahh—as is expected if his name, *Noun-Hhayt,* is understood—loses his adamic quality and sinks into an unevolved state. The relationship between him and Adamah is all to Adamah's advantage. Noahh's consciousness now lapses into the unconsciousness of undifferentiated cosmic life and "uncovers" the true significance of this Noahh whose numbers reveal that he is a life not yet entered into the process of evolution (he falls asleep with his genitals uncovered).

Genesis IX, *22-25.* Hham unexpectedly sees the nudity of his father. He calls his two brothers to come and cover their father, but Noahh curses one of Hham's sons, Canaan, who had never been near him. As is so frequently the case throughout the Bible, the stories of Genesis which appear to be most absurd when traditionally misread turn out when correctly interpreted, to be full of the richest meanings; and this one is no exception. It scarcely needs to be pointed out that if we read the story of Noahh, with the idea that it has to do with real people, it becomes a monstrosity. Here we have a father whose lack of self-respect is such that, being drunk, he lies quite naked. One son, seeing this, is seized with fright and dares not look at his father long enough to cover him. He calls his two brothers who approach backwards, bearing a blanket. The drunkard now regains his senses and launches a malediction. Upon whom? Upon Hham who saw his father's nakedness? Not at all, Noahh curses Canaan, the fourth son of Hham.

No commentator—except in the Qabala—has ever explained this. Thus the story is twisted; and most of its readers think it is Hham who was cursed, which after all would be bad enough. As the letter-numbers give it, the truth of this story is fairly complex. After the Deluge, there is another Genesis: in other words, evolution has ceased because of world destruction and must start again out of a state of primordial life. Noahh, the human germ, symbolically plunged into non-differentiated life, is therefore obliged to re-cover the ground it lost in the Deluge. Notice that this process is strikingly true of life, psychologically speaking. It often happens that although we seem to have evolved towards a true understanding of essentials, we suddenly find ourselves faced with the question on a new and higher level, where we discover that we have really understood nothing at all and consequently have to begin all over again.

Another biological concept that Genesis often presents is that the human "germ" must be constantly prevented from stabilizing itself in a static form of conditioning. Thus it appears that the first-born are the youngest from the standpoint of evolution, because they are the least mature; and conversely, it is the latest born who are endowed with the greatest maturity.* If we assimilate this point of view, we will cease to think of our ancestors as pillars of wisdom and maturity. We will think of them, instead, as representing a younger, more primitive humanity than ours; and we will bestir ourselves to make valid our own more mature vantage point and begin to search for Revelation in ourselves.

* We must keep in mind that the notion is in reference to the general evolution and not to individuals.

We read in the text that Noahh's sons are mentioned in the following order: Sem, Hham and Japhet (Sem and Japhet are the biblical versions). Yet it is clearly stated several times that Japhet, the last named, is big, great. Understanding this and Noahh's state of involution, we can see why Japhet, the "enlarged one", is relegated to the last place; for the exalted one in earthly values is thus the youngest in point of evolution. But Sem, whose *Elohi* is YHWH, is the eldest in point of evolution and therefore inherits the highest rank in the human germ's evolutionary process. The text is very insistent upon the fact that Japhet's is the greatest, though the youngest in maturity. As for Hham, the youngest, he is the second named. In these allegories, the impersonations of no. 2 are always in a dangerous position, the 2 symbolizing the static condition, enclosed in the dwelling of *Bayt* (2). We have seen Hevel dying of it. In this case, Hham (*Hhayt-Mem*), corresponding to the numbers 8.40, is the "son", the exact extension prolongation of Noahh (*Noun-Hhayt*). The process of Noahh Hham is *Noun-Hhayt-Mem*, which is read Nahham, a root which, as often happens in Hebrew, means different things. It can be translated as repentance, pity, consolation or vengeance. It is in any case a fall, a negative movement. When Sem and Japhet arrive, walking backwards, they face evolution and cover the originative, unevolved "father" whose state of being has been defeated and confounded by the great "female", Adamah, because of his having drunk of her "blood", her wine.

When this correct backward direction is taken, Noahh does not really "curse" Canaan (the fourth son of Hham). The word *Arawr*, which has always been translated as "curse", is an extra *Raysh* projected upon *Awr*, the word for light. The reinforced resistance is a multiple of *Raysh*'s already resistant 2. It is the number 4. Noahh projects this onto Hham's fourth son, Canaan, who (symbolically) is thus destined to become the "territory" where Sem must develop.

Mount Ararat, where Noahh's legendary Ark is said to have landed, also has two *Raysh*, meaning two worlds: the temporal

149

and the invisible. In *Arawr* they are copulatively related. It is in this double world, so complex and difficult to grasp (with its doubled resistance) that the human seed entrusted to Sem is sown and must evolve. It implies many deaths but also many stubborn resurrections, many disastrous errors but a tenacious survival.

This biological law is always apparent in the so-called curses of the Bible. It is important to recognize this because once we have freed our mind from the fear of a cursing deity, life stands a chance of being understood.*

It must be added that, according to the code, Canaan is not really supposed to become *a servant of servants to his brethren* (Gen. IX, 25). The schema *Aabd* (70.2.4) indicates a state of conflict between the dauntless 70 and the combined boundaries of 2.4. (*Aabd* was translated "slave" when qualifying Qaheen's relationship with *Adamah*, but slavery always breeds revolt. In Qaheen's case it did; in Canaan's case it also does.)

So the *Arawr* of the repentant Noahh falls upon Canaan whose letter-numbers are 20.50.70.700. They project the seed of life, 50, into the tremendous uncertainty of Qaheen's 7 exalted to the hundreds, that is, into a world that will never afford it any restful shelter. Such has been the blessing of YHWH, all through history on its people. The precision of the symbolic text is such that in Genesis IX, 27, it is said: *Elohim shall enlarge Japhet and he shall dwell in the tents of Sem.* According to the Qabala, Sem, being symbolically the human germ that does not cease its evolution, will assimilate and encompass all the humanisms of our heritage.

We cannot reject the Scriptures, which represent a valid part of this heritage. We must, rather, turn upon them the search-light of impartial investigation, thereby recovering the vital meanings lost in the debacle of mistranslation. As one philoso-

* When the "curse" *Arawr*—1.200.6.200—comes into existence, its *Aleph* (1) becomes 10 and Raysh (200) is alive with Hay (5); thus the Schema becomes 10.5.6.5.: *YHWH.* This identity of a so-called curse and a so-called deity is revealing of the state of psychological fear which underlies the ecclesiastical traditions.

pher puts it, man is "condemned to meaning". We cannot escape the real truths of the Bible, although we have ignored them for so many centuries. To rediscover them now we must, in a way, "walk backwards". We cannot escape because these truths and our own nature are inseparably one.

Genesis xi, *1-8—Babel.* The praiseworthy attempt to become one people and to have one language is shattered (in the translation) by a so-called God who shamelessly declares the malice of his venture. *Let us go down,* says he, *and there confound their language, that they may not understand one another's speech* (Gen. xi, 7).

This shattering of Babel is a direct reference to the necessary hindering of mankind's premature birth, a principle which has been set forth in our preceding chapters. We can therefore assume that Babel is Bible. The original meaning of it had to be confounded and distorted because mankind was not yet sufficiently evolved—not yet ready for the rebirth, or mutation, which the Bible describes as our potential. Does the renaissance of ontological insight in the present-day world indicate an emergent readiness?

19

A Preamble to Genesis XI and XII

THESE CHAPTERS contain a list of Sem's descendants, as far as Abram. From here on, until the close of the fiftieth and last chapter, Genesis becomes a vast epic poem whose meaning has hardly begun to be grasped.

Like a majestic space ship, originating in archetypal spheres, this saga comes down to geographical earth and links itself with history. It embodies all the vital elements, all the archetypes, all the symbols which were described in the preceding chapters. Its extraordinary message is not given in terms of an historical chronicle. In fact, its historical aspects derive from the ontological significance of such names as Abraham, Sarah, Isaac, Rebecca, Jacob and Rachel, as well as such geographic names as Sichem, Moreh, Bethel, Beer-Sheba, Sodom and Gomorrah.

The myth is pre-existent to recorded history. This myth is the condensation in our human societies (pre-human, we prefer to say) of cosmic forces unnoticed by man. We are each one of us a focal point at which energies that pass our understanding meet and function. Due to erroneous self-perception, we struggle perpetually among the contradictions that we engender, attributing to ourselves a false reality.

Were we to follow, step by step, this long saga of Abraham, Isaac and Jacob, it would fill a large volume; and even then it would be useful only to those who have assimilated the ancient code-language of the letter-numbers, of which only the rudiments are given in this book. We shall therefore limit ourselves to a few of the most significant passages.

As a guide for the journey, the symbolic meaning of the

numbers 1, 2 and 3 must be kept firmly in mind. *Number 1*, Abraham, symbolizes the arising or upsurge of the unconditioned germ on its way towards its totally realized human maturity. *Number 2*, his son Isaac, symbolizes the rooting of this germ in a conditioning which if allowed to act, would cause it to come to birth prematurely. *Number 3*, Isaac's son, Jacob, symbolizes the moving forward, biologically, of the germ. In the 1, 2, 3 sequence of this forward movement, the number 2 of the germ, Isaac, is in a very dangerous position! We must grasp this symbolism if we intend to have a notion of what this epic poem conveys. Also, we must remember all the themes which have been expounded from the very outset of this allegory.

The theme of this vast epic poem is the implanting of the human seed, of which the eponymic ancestor is Sem, in the mythical land of Canaan. When YHWH became, through Moses, a tribal deity and the Hebrews forgot the original Revelation, they mistook Canaan for an actual country and waged ruthless wars to conquer it. This is one of the countless examples of the perils inherent in local-temporal interpretation of Scriptures that are universal and timeless in their original import.

20

Abram and Sarai

GENESIS XI. Among the innumerable messages that can be decoded from the Bible's "calculator" the story of Abram is so
important that the three so-called "monotheistic" religions
dutifully consider this personage to be their ancestor. Sem,
the eponymic ancestor of the Semites, is said to have begotten
a son at the age of one hundred (the number symbolizing the
perfection of manhood). The time was two years after the
Deluge, number 2 signifying the "dwelling" or container that
the new seed must build for itself. After the enumeration of
Sem's descendants, we come to old Terahh, Abram's father,
who was of the ninth generation that issued from Sem.

Terahh, with his family and his flocks, lived in "Ur of the
Chaldees", and it was in this land that Abram was born.
Special importance attaches to the name of Abram's birth-
place. This is because the word Ur is, essentially, *Awr*. As you
will remember, *Awr* means light; and the Chaldeans (Kasdeem)
were magicians. So it was in a place that the Bible qualifies as
"light of Magicians" that Abram grew up. The ancient light
of magic handed down from primitive civilizations had come
to a point where it could give birth to a bearer of the inner
light. So far, the light was still uncertain. It did not prove
strong enough for the immediate birth of Elohim's Light. So it
was inevitable that Abram, who was to receive this new Light,
should be removed from Ur.

The epic poem which relates this odyssey is filled with meaning when read according to the numerical-code. Even in the
résumé which follows, this will be apparent. Once upon a time,
in the Land that dwells in the light of Magicians, the seed of

humanity under this magic light emphasized the number 70: the safeguard of every unconditioned human possibility. Seventy then brought forth the number 3 (Terahh begat three sons "at the age of 70"), three roots by which the seed sought to take form. But since in the "light of the Magicians" the third seed could not mature, it died. (Gen. XI, 28: And Haran died before his father Terahh in the land of his nativity, in Ur of the Chaldees.) Seed number 2 (Nahhor) went its own way. Seed number 1 (Abram) had to be saved—that is to say, rescued from the static subhuman order of things, where magic over-powered the bodies and ruled the minds.

So the impersonation of no. 70 took this one root which was left and saved it by leaving Ur of the Chaldees with its static light of magic and moved towards the land of strife and pain and joy and great uncertainty and total insecurity, where the seed of humanity must take root if it is to survive and come to maturity: Canaan.

They never went beyond *Hharan* and old *Terahh* died there at the age of two hundred and five. Or, to be more accurate, I should say that the schema *Terahh* consumes itself in the schema *Hharan* as can be seen by comparing the cogent numbers: 400.200.8—8.200.700.

It is interesting to compare the name of *Haran* who *died before his father Terahh in the land of his nativity, in Ur of the Chaldees* (Gen. XI, 28) with the name of *Hharan* of the place where Terahh died. It is of extreme interest to study the story of *Lot*, son of that *Haran* who died where he was born, and the story of *Sodom* and *Gomorrah*. The words ascribed to YHWH when assigning his mission to Abram, *Lekh-Lekha*, have also great significance. Those narratives are inexhaustible in meaningful details.

Abram having gone back to *Ur* leaves at last definitely, with his wife Sarai and his nephew *Lot and the souls that they had gotten* (Gen. XII, 5) and they reach Canaan. The name of that symbolic earth is the equation, the solution of which Abram has the mission to bring about. It is the land of all the conflicts of the world, of all violences, of all impediments to freedom. And it is in the midst of it that Abram is committed to sow the seed of the human-to-be.

That germ will have to take root in Canaan and, paradoxically, will have to avoid remaining fixed in it. It will have, under the sign of no. 3, to conquer the duality symbolized by that earth. In the midst of cruel battles it will have to learn how not to battle, because taking part with one or other of the contestants would prevent its ripening.

Thus begin the adventures of Abram the initiate. It is the story of the greatest conquest that mankind must achieve.

In Canaan Abram starts on his mission with the action of no. 3: he builds three altars to YHWH: two upon his arrival, one later on. The first altar is mentioned in verse no. 7. *Abram* builds it *unto the plain of Moreh* (*Mem-Waw-Raysh-Hay*: 40.6, 200.5). He builds the second between *Beth-El* (the house of Elohim) and *Aai* (*Ayn-Yod*: 70.10).

Under the impact of these first intrusions into its passivity, Canaan reacts and resists: there is a famine.

Abram and Sarai are obliged to "go down" into Egypt, the name of which is Mitsraim, symbolizing (as shown by its letter-numbers) the fat, female earth with its rich, physiological substance. Now we come to Abram's apparently insane statement that Sarai is his sister. She is kidnapped by Pharaoh; and when Pharaoh learns that she is Abram's wife, he gives her back to him and exclaims (paraphrased): "Why did you say she is your sister and not your wife? I would have left her alone! Now take her, and go away, both of you!"

Here again we see that it is in the most absurd passages that we may find the most important lessons. Abram wishes to elevate woman to the free rank of a "sister"; he wishes her status to equal his, so that she can become his companion, fully collaborating with him. He does not wish woman to remain merely at the level of a concubine in a harem. Sarai, however, does not understand; and in the land of carnal appetites, she yields in the manner of a mere creature of the flesh.

Genesis XIII. Through this adventure—resulting from the woman's lack of maturity—Abram's terrestial wealth increases (we can meditate upon, and verify this fact every day). In Canaan, however, work awaits him. Abram returns to the place where he had built his second altar. This is between *Bayt-El* and a place whose numbers are 70.10: *Aai* (you remember the significance of 70). This is the place where Lot and Abram separate. Lot is attracted by what the numbers describe as a well-watered plain, and he goes towards Sodom and Gomorrah.

The difference between the name *Sodom* and the name *Adam* lies in the fact that Sodom has in it no *Aleph*; this is replaced by *Sammekh*, with the numerical significance of 60. Thus the blood of Sodom—unlike that of Adam, which is *"Aleph"* in the blood —is incapable of sublimation. Gomorrah is synonymous with slavery.

Abram, failing to vitalize Lot, is now free and can retire into *Mamre, which is in Hebron* (these names need not be explained here), where he builds the third altar to YHWH.

In fact he inserts the no. 3 (Gen. XIII, 18). He fertilizes the two *Mem* of *Mamre* (*Mem-Mem-Raysh-Aleph*) by enlarging them to the cosmic level Raysh, whereby Aleph springs forth. Hebron, or rather Hhevron (8.2.200.6.700) is a primordial state of energy elevated to the highest cosmic exponent 700.

Genesis XIV. The story of the war between the four kings is too long to tell here. But it is a phase necessary to the fulfilment of Abram's mission.

Genesis XV. The symbolic episode of cutting the carcasses of different animals in halves and the burning fire which passes between them is also too long to relate. It is a test, which Abram passes successfully. YHWH then makes a covenant with Abram and "gives" him, or rather says that he gives him, all the land between Egypt and the Euphrates.

The myth, at this point, tends more and more to materialize into geographical realities and its language accompanies it, so to speak, in making this "landing". The original schemata become real persons and the cosmic energy, designated as YHWH, becomes a divinity.*

Genesis XVI. Sarai now brings her servant woman, Hagar, to Abram; and this Egyptian handmaid becomes pregnant. She despises Sarai and taunts her with being a barren wife. Sarai is angry. This servant has no intelligence; she is just an animal, passive and subjugated as are all the Egyptian women Sarai has seen. Sarai discharges her, and Hagar is greatly afflicted.

YHWH comforts her and tells her the exact opposite of what is related in our translations, where he is supposed to say to *Hagar* (Gen. XVI, 12) that *Ishmael,* her son (eponymous ancestor of the Arabs), *will be a wild man; his hand will be against everyman and every man's hand against him,* whereas he actually says that *Ishmael will be a prolific Adam, his hand with all and the hands of all with him.*

This utterance to a prolific woman is logical. But Sarai is fore-ordained to a different destiny: she must develop her intelligence and give birth to a germ that will for ever continue its growth. It will not yield to any conditionings inviting it to become a lateral branch of the tree of life. Through cruel pains and sorrows it will have to learn how to become indeterminate even to its own perception.

* The cabalists have never anthropomorphized YHWH or Elohim. Their symbolical language has led the non-initiates astray. According to the fundamental textbook of Qabala, *Sepher Yetsira,* Abram owes his revelation to his intelligent study of the structure of energy.

21

Circumcision
(Genesis XVII, 10-15)

Thus Sarai attains the perfection that is required of her. She reaches it at an age symbolizing the perfection of woman: 90 years. At the same time Abram reaches the symbolic age of perfection in man: 100 years. YHWH then reveals to Abram his mission, and Elohim confers upon him a new life. This is symbolized by a new syllable in his name: *Thy name shall be Abraham* (Gen. xvii, 5). Immediately, there follows, clearly and explicitly stated, the covenant of circumcision.

It appears as a covenant not between YHWH and Abraham, but between Elohim and Abraham, and it is only after its establishment that Sarai's name is changed to Sarah.

Circumcision at eight days is generally considered a hygienic measure, though actually something far more important is involved: the transformation of the human body. The rationale is the need to sever manhood (as typified by Adam) from the purely animal heritage through a process of sublimation and transformation.

In the biblical allegory, we have seen Esha in the Garden of Eden taking the initiative in man's sensorial and cerebral development. As we shall see later on—with Sarah, Rebecca, Rachel and Mary-mother-of-Jesus—the human germ develops into manhood if the woman is able to sublimate the primordial female within herself. But the fact of circumcision in the human male actually makes a profound contribution to the development of woman. It affects both sexes, physiologically and psychologically.

This shock is deeply felt by the individual. Undergone eight days after birth, as it is among the Jews, its effects are so decisive within the structure of the unconscious and the vital centres that it is justifiable to find in circumcision a factor of the exceptional history of the Jews. We may well suppose that those who instituted this practice did so with a specific goal in view. Circumcision intensifies the development of the sensorial apparatus through an effective co-ordination of sensory activity; it awakens the intellectual faculties; the sexual energy is utilized by the body prior to the awakening of sex.

The result is a freer self which transforms and assimilates the elements of its environment according to the needs of its own individual development. At the same time this self is carried along by the inner movement which engenders that faculty of assimilation. The individual is in perfect harmony with the rapid changes of the world.

These remarks may give insight into the manner in which the vital and contradictory movement set up in the human process by the circumcision is considered, in mythical terms, as a "pact" with Elohim (which is this process). This pact causes the movement of the universe to penetrate into the very flesh of the body, and into the mind as well. In fact, it has "conquered the flesh" by obliging it to transmute, to transfigure, itself.

This is a theme already familiar to us; the transmutation of what is fixed and static (in this case, the flesh, the blood, the "dam" of Adam), so that it can eventually allow the life of *Aleph* to be resuscitated.*

* For further elaboration upon the subject, see Note 2, "Circumcision," p. 221.

22

From Sarah to Rebecca

GENESIS XVIII, 12. *Sarah laughed to herself, saying, After I am grown old shall I have pleasure, my Lord being old also?* The Hebrew text states later on that Isaac, her future son, is *Yitzhhaq*: he who laughs. And we shall see that his life is, for the most part, a comedy.

We can pass over the sordid story of *Lot*, remembering chiefly that this schema (*Lammed-Waw-Tav*: 50.6.400) is fore-doomed. His wife does not even have a name. Looking *back from behind him* (Gen. XIX, 26) she becomes *a pillar of salt*. His two daughters who sleep with him when he is drunk are symbolic. The ignominious decline of *Lot* as an archetype is a consequence of his weakness.

Genesis xx, *1*. Abraham sojourns between *Qadesh* and *Shur* (between 100.4.300 and 300.6.200). These numbers show a balancing or rhythm, from the cosmic *Aleph* (100) to its metabolism (300) and back to the universal "container", 200.

We now come upon a second episode dealing with a kidnapped woman: *And Abraham said of Sarah his wife, She is my sister: and Abimelekh King of Gerar sent and took Sarah* (Gen. xx, 2).

But womanhood has progressed and, in contrast to her experience with Pharaoh, *Sarah* successfully passes the test. *Abimelekh* has a dream in which *Elohim* says to him: *Thou art but a dead man, for the woman which thou hast taken: for she is a man's wife.* So he does not come near her.

Genesis xx, *12*. Abraham reveals, or suggests, that *Sarah* is his sister because they both have the same "father". But—adds *Abraham*—she is not *Imi*'s daughter. In a restricted sense, *Imi* means "my mother". *Abram* however, according to Qabala, declares himself here, *Ben-Adam*, son of Adam, just as Jesus did, at a much later date. And the very important fact is that he includes *Sarah* in that denomination, thereby acknowledging her spiritual elevation.

Genesis xx, *16*. *Abimelekh* makes atonement to *Abraham* with a *thousand pieces of silver*. One thousand is the most exalted state of *Aleph* (the word Aleph actually means one thousand in Hebrew). Symbolically this means that *Abraham*'s undertaking is successful.

Genesis xxi, *1*. *And the Lord visited Sarah as he had said, and the Lord did unto Sarah as he had spoken*. Can it be said more clearly that it was YHWH (mistranslated "the Lord") who engendered *Isaac*, *Sarah*'s son?

All dogmatic faith being laid aside, this verse must be understood as it is written. Is it necessary to state that the "mystery of Incarnation" through Mary-mother-of-Jesus is neither unique nor even original?

This point is so important that one of Qabala's most fundamental postulates must here be insisted on: YHWH is not a deity. We have often said that, according to Qabala, the real mystery which it is totally impossible to understand is, simply, existence. Any deistic notion serves to remove from the mind, by means of fallacious explanations, the disturbing realization of that all-invading immediacy.

The natural supports of these devices are omnipotent deities, because in fairy tales magic wands are their own explanations: magic is magic and God is almighty, and for many that is enough.

This verse does not claim a priority for Sarah's pregnancy through "the Lord". When YHWH ceases to be anthropomorphized, *Sarah* and *Yitzhhaq*, and for that matter *Abraham*, must solely be a set of schemata, or formulas, expressing different states of energy. They must abandon the human shapes that the psyches have kept alive, as complexes, through many centuries, with the obstinate—and unconscious—purpose of not wishing to understand them.

Between YHWH as a "Lord" and *Sarah* as a woman, the "doing unto her as he had spoken" loses its meaning. The text actually reads: *Ve-YHWH Paqad Et Sarah.* The schema *Paqad* (80.100.4) shows that in the primordial unstructured energy (80) the cosmic *Aleph* (100) creates a resistance (4) that sets it in biological motion. In terms of psychology it can be said that this is an awakening of the subconscious and unconscious strata. It is given to that part of symbolic womanhood which is in everyone of us, whether female or male.

Let us now consider the schemata *Abram* and *Abraham*, *Sarai* and *Sarah*. In *Genesis* XVII, *5* (5 is *Hay*) *Abram* had been given an extra life *Hay* (5) when a covenant was established between him and YHWH. This means that the *Aleph-Bayt* (Ab) of *Ab-Ram*, representing the entire Alphabet of that initiate's knowledge, became creative. Its action upon Ram became alive as shown by the *Hay* (5) being introduced between *Raysh* and *Mem*. So whereas *Abram* is 1.2.200.40, *Abraham* is 1.2.200.5.40, thus allowing the final *Mem* to become 600. The perfect *Abraham* is therefore 1.2.200.5.600.

In *Genesis* XVII, *15* (3 × 5) *Sarai* became *Sarah*. The schema *Sarai*: 300.200.10 was transformed into 300.200.5 which means that the existential *Yod* (10) of *Sarai* is, in *Sarah*, the *Hay* (5) of life.

Genesis XXI, *2* to *Genesis* XXV, *20* contains so much significant detail that it should be read attentively. Briefly, here are some of the episodes it relates: the second expulsion of *Hagar*; the well of *Beer-sheba* (the word *Sheba* means seven); the long discussion between *Abraham* and *Abimelekh* concerning a *well of water*; *Abraham*'s gift to *Abimelekh* of *seven ewe lambs* as token of his good faith (as always, the number 7 is associated with *Abraham*'s actions); the so-called sacrifice of *Isaac*, which finally was not required (it was another instance of YHWH's testing, as happened in the case of *Jacob*, and of *Moses*); the *four hundred shekels of silver* paid for *Sarah*'s place of burial by *Abraham*; the hesitations as to the land where the human seed, *Isaac*, should be given in custody; the choice of the woman who, next, should carry forward the lineage of exalted womanhood; *Rebekah* drawing water plentifully from the well; and the proof that *Rebekah* had reached the stage of feminine transfiguration required of her before she could become *Isaac*'s wife (Gen. XXIV, 29: *And Rebekah had a brother*, meaning that she had attained the "rank" of sister). Then another long description of *Rebekah* drawing water at the well; and finally, the significant statement when *Rebekah*'s mother and brother joins her father at the moment of *Rebekah*'s departure: *And they sent away Rebekah, their sister.... And they blessed Rebekah, and said unto her: Thou art our sister (Gen. XXIV, 59-60).*

Genesis XXIV, 67 relates an incident which, considered psychoanalytically, shows a regressive tendency in the character of *Isaac* (he being the number 2 of the lineage *Abraham, Isaac, Jacob*). *And Isaac brought her into his mother Sarah's tent, and took Rebekah, and she became his wife: and he loved her: and Isaac was comforted after his mother's death.* Love for the mother here appears as a symptom of regression.

This transference is well known today and was certainly understood by the authors of Genesis because nothing could better describe *Isaac* being no. 2. The schemata, ideograms, numbers, symbols in this text confer on the myth a psychological meaning parallel to its factual narration. When discovered in the depth of our beings, it can well strike us as being a revelation.

Genesis can thus be read at four different levels: the anecdote, the symbol, the ontology and finally at a level which transcends speech and cannot be communicated.

We will later quote and comment upon *Genesis* XXV relating *Abraham*'s death, *Ishmael*'s posterity and *Isaac*'s two sons. First an important event must be mentioned: *Isaac*'s dwelling in *Gerar*. It is one of the important parts in Genesis, where the revelation most deeply resides. We will only consider the first twelve verses of that chapter.

Genesis XXVI, *1-12: the anecdote.* There is a famine and YHWH appears unto *Isaac*, forbids him to go to Egypt, and promises a blessing if he remains in the land. *Isaac* obeys and dwells in

Gerar. And the men of the place asked him about his wife and he said she is my sister, for he feared to say she is my wife lest the men of the place should kill me on account of Rebekah (verse 7).

However, *Abimelekh*, through his window, sees *Isaac* and *Rebekah* talking and joking together. He calls *Isaac* and says to him: *Certainly she is thy wife, and how hast thou said: She is my sister?*

Isaac answers: *Because I said: Lest I die on account of her.* And *Abimelekh* says: *What is this thou hast done unto us? Almost had one of the people* copulated with her (I must forgo the prudish "married" of my English Bible).

Such is the hopelessly absurd anecdote. Once already, when in Egypt, *Abram* had said of *Sarai*: she is my sister, and Pharaoh had slept with her. Then, realizing the truth, he had angrily returned her to *Abram*. A second time, *Abraham*, in *Gerar*, had said of *Sarah*: She is my sister, and *Abimelekh*, warned in a dream, averted just in time the widespread calamity which would have fallen upon his kingdom had he taken *Sarah*.

And now, in the same *Gerar*, *Isaac* repeats to the same *Abimelekh*—who has not forgotten his former narrow escape— the same old insane story. But this time. *Abimelekh*, looking out of his window, actually sees that *Isaac* and *Rebekah* are man and wife, and the danger thus avoided is such that he orders: *He that touches this man and his wife shall be put to death.*

The very inconsistency of those stories solicits our attention. Were *Isaac*'s fears simply unjustified, there would perhaps be some sense in declaring *Rebekah* his sister, but his utterances clearly appear as a diabolical trap set for the purpose of destroying *Abimelekh*'s entire kingdom.

It has already been said, concerning the *Abram* and *Abraham* episodes, that in the second one *Sarah* is not taken, which means that the symbolical woman, typified by her, has evolved. In the third adventure, *Rebekah* openly, in public, conversing pleasantly with *Isaac*, declares herself to be fully adult and free. She is on a level with her husband, a companion, a "sister" to him. We have now to examine the symbols.

Genesis XXVI, *1-12: the symbols. Isaac*'s sojourn in *Gerar* cannot be understood symbolically unless examined in the general context of the myth. We must therefore summarize the symbols concerning that narrative from *Abram* on.

Awr-Kasdeem (1.6.200—20.300.4.10.40): the light of magicians.

Terahh (400.200.8): *Abram*'s father. Just as *Noahh* (50.8) this schema is symbolic of the ending of a cycle. The cosmic resistance 400.200 that has animated it returns to no. 8, the reservoir of undifferentiated energy.

Abram (1.2.200.40) becoming *Abraham* (1.2.200.5.600): the initiate propelled by a renewal of energy 1.2 and acting upon the cosmic "house" 200, conferring upon it a new life, 5.

Nahhor (50.8.6.200) *Abram*'s "brother", his counterpart. This schema symbolizes a life in existence (50) reverted to its primordial state (8) and fertilizing the 200 from within. The direction of that flow of life is opposite to that of *Abraham*.

Haran (5.200.700) is a premature birth having no viability. Its 5 is lost in 200 and is projected in 700 without having matured. It "dies" in the presence of its father, in its place of birth.

Remember that *Terahh* "aged 70" gives birth to no. 3 (three sons). But the "Light of Magicians" is not enough. It cannot guide the human seed towards the light that it carries within itself.

Canaan (20.50.70.700) is the place (20) full of existential life (50) where all the uncertainties, all the creations and dissolutions, all the discoveries, inventions, buildings and shattering disruptions of structures must perforce happen (70 and 700). It is in the midst of that turmoil that the human seed can and must evolve and grow. It must never allow itself to rest because if it is not active it regresses. The symbol *Canaan* is over the whole planet in every conflict, in every tragic error as in every beautiful and transient achievement. In it, mankind must come to understand its cosmic significance.

We cannot, in this essay, go into the vast epic poem of that spiritual conquest, symbolized in the deeds of *Abraham, Isaac* and *Jacob*. Its decoding would take far more space than could be devoted to it in this book. Every name of person or place, every action, contention, truce or covenant has its inner meaning and should be examined with care.

Abraham and *Sarah* at the respective ages of 100 and 90 symbolize with those numbers perfect manhood and perfect womanhood. The extra *Hay* (5) granted to *Abram* and *Sarai* is the proof of it.

Abimelekh (1.2.10.40.30.500). Literally: "my father King" is the symbol of temporal sovereignty. He has the knowledge of *Aleph-Bayt* and the power of unchallenged rulers. Those rulers can bestow their grace at the call of YHWH whose servants they are. They can also at his call throw their might into the balance and annihilate the people, as had *Neb-u-khad-nez-zar* in Jerusalem by the *wrath* of YHWH (Chr. II, 16-17).

Yitzhhaq (10.90.8.100) the no. 2 of the *Abraham-Isaac-Jacob* triad. This schema is a paradox. Essentially it belongs to a triune movement. In its physical disposition it is twofold, and has to be so, as a link between the conqueror 3 and the conquered 2 (duality as symbolized by *Canaan*). Its structure is ingenious. Its 8, between 90 and 100, is almost farcical. No wonder that Yitzhhaq means "he laughs".

But the 3 in disguise, the comedy, the laughter are playing a deadly serious game, at its most critical stage. *Isaac* must give birth to *Israel*. In his schema is the seed of man-made-perfect, but in such a condition as to have no possibility of action. *Yitzhhaq* is a paradoxical balance of a pre-evolved 8 and a totally evolved (female and male) 90 and 100. In this schema the beginning is included in the end: the entire evolutionary process is out of its range. So *Yitzhhaq* is in a state of paralysis: *his eyes were dim* says the text (Gen. XXVII, 1) but we are not compelled to believe it. His blindness is the pretence of a helpless man. His helplessness however is dramatically true. Anybody acting from out of the current trend of existence can give a shattering blow to this strange state of neutrality between a

167

pre-structured energy (8) and a total maturity (90.100). And *Isaac* in *Gerar* knows it. Any man, in whatever condition, can destroy him by simply touching him. He also knows that the human-to-be is entirely in the care of womanhood. If *Rebekah* is not, symbolically, his "sister", his companion, and if she does not take upon herself the task of rescuing the precious seed within Jacob, the evolution of man is doomed.

Abimelekh is aware. He knows. Hence his drastic order: not only *Rebekah*, but also *Isaac* must not be touched!

Genesis XXVI, *1-12: the ontological meaning.* The key to this "sisterhood" is in the schema *Ehhot* (*Aleph-Hhayt-Tav*: 1.8.400) which means "sister", although in the Hebrew language, sister is spelt *Aleph-Hhayt-Waw-Tav* (1.8.6.400). This addition of *Waw* converts the schema into a purely physical classification.

Ehhot is a simple formula. Its 8, between *Aleph* and *Tav* is everything that *Aleph* must impregnate. We must keep in mind *Aleph* in fullness (*Aleph-Lammed-Phay*: 1.30.80). Its action is the biosphere's metabolism. It is the creation of living beings following cosmic nuptials, always referred to by Qabala either as *Awr* (light) in physical appearance, or otherwise.

In the metaphysical sphere of our present narrative, we use a direct relationship between the 10.90.8.100 of *Yitzhhaq* and the 1.8.400 of *Ehhot*, and we have come to understand that ontologically *Ehhot* is not a sister, but *Aleph*'s spouse. *Aleph* is timeless, *Ehhot* is of time. To become spiritually pregnant means, for her, initiative, action, freedom, self-reliance. The centrifugal male energy can sow the seed of illumination; its structure depends on the centripetal energy building it in its right direction. Then the "spouse" is "sister".

Yitzhhaq is supposed to fear *lest the man of the place should kill* (him) *for Rebekah* (Gem. XXVI, 7). What he says in fact is: *Pen Yehregouni Anshi Hamaqom Aal Rivqah.* In numbers: 80.700—10.5.200.3.50.10—1.50.300.10—5.40.100.6.40—70.30—200.2.100.5.

By which he means: my unformulated (80) energy is lost in the (700) cosmic indetermination. The existent (10) life (5) of the universe (200) must be organic (3) so as to be realized (50) in existence (10). This must be done by *Aleph* (1) alive (50) acting through the breath of *Elohim* (300) so as to come into existence (10). Then, and then only can life (5) act upon matter (40) so as to allow the cosmic *Aleph* (100) to impregnate (6) matter (40), which means conferring the sanctified 70 to organic energy (30). This would be a projection of the universal 200 into the individual 2 and the individual would emit (put forth) the cosmic Aleph (100) alive (5)!

This last schema 200.2.100.5 is none other than *Rivqah* (*Rebekah*). Its utterance in six words is a complete metaphysical *exposé*.

Lastly there is the pseudo-window through which *Abimelekh* sees the couple. This symbolic king typifying all temporal sovereigns looks *Beaad Hahhalon* (2.70.4—5.8.30.6.700), translated "from the window". It is true that *Aad* can mean "from", but it also means "eternity"; and *Hhalon* can mean "window" but the same root *Hhiloni* means "secular". Cabalists have almost constantly resorted to such double meanings. We must understand here that Abimelekh, symbol of worldly power, looks upon the couple that symbolizes the totality of universal life from his "secular eternity". Through him and her, talking pleasantly together, he has the vision of what she really is: spouse, not sister when men and women are considered as projections of cosmic energy.

The text says: *Yitzhhaq Metzahheq Et Rivqah Ishtou*: he laughs, he jests with her. There is in that description a sense of relaxation, a communion in a happy state of achievement that no translation can render truly. Abimelekh's clear awareness of it is an extraordinary blending of eternal structured energy as time and duration, and of eternal timelessness.

Genesis xxvi, *1-12: the ineffable*. The direct understanding in one single act of perception of the above three spheres can clarify to the reader what the Revelation really is.

Genesis xxv, *21-23: Yitzhhaq* addresses a prayer to *YHWH* because *Rivqah* is barren. The prayer is listened to favourably.

Rivqah conceives twins who struggle together within her. She says: *If so, why this my desire?* And she questions YHWH.

Rivqah is barren and YHWH intervenes, as *Sarah* was barren and YHWH intervened. *Rachel* will have to wait 7 years and 7 again. This insistently deferred action illustrates not only the necessary procrastination of Genesis where the human germ is concerned but also its intimate relationship to YHWH.

In answer to *Rivqah*'s question, YHWH reveals to her that two *Goim* (nations) are within her (the narrative is thus clearly in the sphere of phylogenesis) and that *the elder shall serve the younger.*

This is a reference to a recurrent theme: in the genealogical tree of mankind extending through many centuries, the first born are the least evolved, because they are the youngest, the furthest from maturity.

We know that *Rivqah*'s first-born is *Yissav* (Esau). He will therefore have to submit to the second-born, the elder *Yaaqov* (Jacob). *Rivqah* understands the message as we also must learn to understand it.

The schemata of the two brothers identifies them completely. *Yissav* (70.300.6) is all possibles (70) acting through the cosmic metabolism (300) genetically (6). *Yaaqov* (10.70.100.2) is essentially different. His 70 is the result of a rooting in existence (10). It brings forth a cosmic *Aleph* (100) and projects it in *Bayt* (2), the individual "container".

These schemata may be a surprise to those who remember the description of *Esau*, heavy, hairy, earthly, and of *Jacob*, weak and meditative, but it must not be forgotten that at this point in the narrative one of the two brothers must personify no. 3 and thrust roots into *Canaan*: *Canaan* being the world at large with its miseries, its exploitations, and its struggles for freedom. The seed of the human-to-be must not and cannot establish itself in any given condition. It must be adaptable and unadapted; it must be in this world and above it, as swift as the flow of contingencies so as neither to rot in dead waters nor be overrun.

Yissav's possibilities (70) are carried away, blown around in the uncertainties of the universal flow of life (300). He is too primitive, too raw to find in himself enough strength to build a resistance to life. He will be prolific (6) and that is all that is to be said for him at the moment.

Yaakov's 70, on the contrary, is fully existent in between 10 and 100. All his energy is concentrated in 2, his *Bayt*: the building of a strong individuality. The text says that his is *Tam* (400.40). This is a remarkable schema. It expresses the greatest possible resistance to life, both in a cosmic sense (400) and existentially (40). Only a great intensity of life can be in need of such a resistance. The word *Tam* in Hebrew means innocence, simplicity, sincerity, integrity, and it is said (Gen. xxv, 27) that *Jacob* is a simple man, living in his tent, whereas *Esau* is a great hunter and a worker in the fields.

Before coming to the contentious "dish of lentils", the "selling" of *Esau*'s birthright, and the lives of the two brothers a few words must be added concerning their parents.

Rivqah (200.2.100.5). As we have seen her she is accomplished, transfigured. She will be ordained YHWH's agent of a sacred transmission through *Jacob*, which will deprive him of all his father's earthly possessions in favour of *Esau*. It must be noted that *Rivqah* is the only one to converse with YHWH.

The traditional well-known story is as follows: *Isaac* is prepared to give his blessing to *Esau* but *Rivqah* disguises *Jacob*, sends him to his old and blind father so as to deceive him, and *Isaac* blesses *Jacob* believing that it is *Esau*.

What is less known is that *Isaac* is acting a part: he is not deceived, he is a willing accomplice. Let us read the details of that blessing.

Yitzhhaq calls "his son" *Yissav* and tells him: *I am old, I know not the day of my death* (Gen. xxvii, 2). He sends him out to hunt and asks him to cook a savoury dish of venison, *that my soul may bless thee before I die.*

And Rebecca heard when Isaac spake to Esau his son. . . . And Rebecca spake unto Jacob her son. . . . The text insists on saying that

171

Esau is *Isaac*'s son whereas Jacob is *Rebecca*'s son. She informs *Jacob* of what *Isaac* has said to *Esau* and tells him to fetch *two good kids*. She will *make them into a savoury meat* that *Jacob* will bring to *Isaac*, so as to receive the blessing intended for *Esau*.

Jacob answers that his brother is *Sayir* (hairy) (300.70.10.200) whereas he is *Hhalaq* (8.30.100) (Gen. XXVII, 11). These schemata have a double meaning: *Sayir* also means that *Esau* is carried away as by a tempest—and in analysing his name we have seen that it is so: he cannot take root in *Canaan*. *Hhalaq* besides meaning *I am a smooth man*, expresses the fact the *Yaakov* is helpless: he has no means of action.

And *Jacob* goes on to say: *My father peradventure will feel me and I shall seem to him as a deceiver; and I shall bring a curse upon me and not a blessing*. But answers *Rebecca: Upon me be the curse, my son.* . . .

The schema translated "curse" is *Qlalah* (100.30.30.5). The root *Qof-Lammed-Lammed* is another example of ambiguity in the Hebrew language. In colloquial Hebrew it means (pronounced *Qilel*) "curse", but its double *Lammed* following *Qof* expresses a double organic movement issuing from the cosmic *Aleph*, so swift and dynamic that we can well understand its impact being felt as a "curse" by the psyche. The schema *Barakah*, translated "blessing", is exactly *Qlalah*'s opposite. Its numbers 2.200.20.5 describe a happy and completely static life in which the psyche can rest and slumber.

Rivqah's utterance, when decoded, reveals itself to be in the core of the myth and of *Yaaqov*'s action in it: "I take upon me", she says, "your *Qof* (cosmic *Aleph*) and its dual functional energy."

It is to be noted that *Yitzhhaq*, *Rivqah* and *Yaaqov*, all three have the *Qof* (100). According to the cabalistic rationalization, one *Qof* is enough, two would propel anyone beyond our tangible universe. So *Rivqah* must take *Yaaqov*'s *Qof* upon herself, she must denude her son, send him deprived of what he essentially is. He must be totally empty so as to be in disguise and receive his *Barakah*.

When we really consider the words "upon me be the curse",

we see that they have no meaning, because there is no curse. When we consider *Qlalah* according to code, and do not read *Qilel* (the Hebrew for curse), we can meditate upon the deep general meaning of that narrative and discover its beauty.

And here is the comedy: *Rivqah* dresses up *Yaaqov* in *Yissav*'s best clothes and covers his hands and neck with the skin of the kids. And when thus attired *Jacob* presents a dish to his father. *Isaac* asks him who he is (why ask if he thinks he knows it is *Esau*?). *Jacob* answers that he is *Esau* and that this is the venison. Isaac asks *How is it that thou hast found it so quickly? Jacob* answers that it was given by YHWH-*Elohim*. *Isaac* feels him so (he says) as to be sure that it is Esau. He actually feels the hands covered with kid skin and says: *The voice is Jacob's voice, but the hands are the hands of Esau* (Gen. XXVII, 22).

What an incredible statement! *Isaac* has recognized *Jacob*'s voice and blind or not he cannot possibly have mistaken a piece of lamb's skin hastily put upon a hand for a hand, however hairy.

Not only is he not deceived but his declaration is so obviously a make-believe that there must be a powerful psychological reason for the persistence of the belief in this deception.

We hope to uncover gradually the reason in the next chapter. We can state it as being our conclusion: *Jacob*, whose real name, *Israel*, will be revealed, has inspired fear in the hearts of millions.

When *Esau* returns from his hunting he cries out bitterly because *Jacob* has received the blessing of the first-born of YHWH. *Bless me, even me also O my father*, says he. And *Isaac* gives him the blessing that will bestow on him all the richness of the earth (Gen. XXVII, 39-40).

Behold, thy dwelling shall be the fatness of the earth and the dew of heaven from above. And by the sword shalt thou live and shalt serve thy brother: and it shall come to pass when thou shalt have the dominion, that thou shalt break his yoke from off thy neck.

And because *Esau* inherits all the riches and all the power on earth, he hates *Jacob* and plans to kill him. When summoned by

173

his mother, *Jacob* prepares to escape. He then again meets *Isaac*, undisguised this time, and *Isaac*, suddenly not too old to understand nor too blind to see (he will live many more years) instructs him clearly and in detail as to where he must go and as to what he must do, and he endows him with great authority as *Abraham's* successor.

23

Jacob and Esau

THE QUESTION as to who is legally the elder of twins has often been discussed. To my knowledge many judgments have considered it to be the second to emerge from the womb.

But the strife between *Jacob* and *Esau* has nothing to do with genetics. It is on an ontological level. Its far-reaching drama so vividly portrayed is a projection, on the psychological and pseudo-historical level, of one of the most important themes of Genesis: the conflict between YHWH and the earth as to who is the bearer of the evolutionary human seed: YHWH's son or the earth's son?

Those two symbolical descendants are perpetually battling in the individual and collective subconscious—alas too often the winner emerges as *Esau*.

In the narrative the conflict is centred upon the schema *Adam: Aleph-Dallet-Mem*: or *Aleph* in *Dam* (blood). In which of the two brothers is the seed of *Aleph*'s resurrection?

As in every one of its essential points the significance of this narrative is hidden in words having a double meaning. *Adam* means red and presently we shall even see it translated as "pottage"!

In Genesis xxv, 25, *Esau* is thus described: *The first came out red all over like an hairy garment.* In Hebrew: *We-Yotsey Harishon Admoni Kelou Kiaderet Saar.*

We have already met the root *Yotsey* when, on the "third day", the earth *Totsey* (produces) its vegetation in its limited response to the cosmic flow of unlimited energy *Tadshey*. We said that this reponse is a non-resistance, a yielding, a bringing

175

fruit in which the *Dallet* of human resistance to life is eliminated in exchange for the proliferating *Waw*. The schema *Yotsey* clearly qualifies *Esau* as being a product of the earth.

The schema *Admoni*, translated "red", is *Adam* with the addition of *Waw-Noun-Yod* (6.50.10) which confirms humanity as being prolific flesh in existence. As to the schema *Saar* (300.70.200) we have already said that it expresses a kind of tempest, sweeping *Esau* away in the cosmic metabolism.

Esau's rough appearance and his rustic pursuits seem to contradict the idea of his being carried away in the cosmos, but suggests rather that his taking root in the land contradicts the human necessity of taking a firm hold upon the swiftly moving world in the process of which lies his own gestation. *Esau*, in the primitive state of humanity intimately involved in nature, is obviously related to the cosmic metabolism, but as a product of the earth he "yields", whereas the true *Adam* "resists" and develops his individuality.

So *Yissav* is an *Adam* produced by the earth. As such his appearance is "adamic" meaning simply "red".

It is an exhilarating experience to enter into this dramatic confrontation, to live it in one's own self. *Isaac* in the guise of an earthly father, receives from the earth (*Adamah*) a son. He is the best and only *Adam* she can produce, but he is spurious as compared to the real archetype.

Is it simply a comedy? Or, rather, are we not called upon here to be witnesses of a blending, a symbiosis between two vital currents of the one living energy manifesting itself in opposite directions so as to assert itself by its own negation?

Esau smells wholly of good earth. His *is as the smell of a field which YHWH has blessed* (Gen. xxvii, 27). He is powerful, violent and he knows how to hate. *Esau* is repeatedly said to be *Edom* (1.4.6.40): an *Adam* in which is introduced the copulative *Waw* of proliferation. And who is *Edom*? Genesis xxxvi gives the generations of *Esau who is Edom: their riches were more than that they might dwell together*. They were leaders and mighty kings, and do we not know the famous descendant *Herod* who swore to murder all the newborn males so as not to miss murdering Jesus?

As to *Yaaqov* all that need be added here to his description concerns the root *Aaqov* (70.100.2), which has as many meanings in Hebrew as *Jacob* has ways and means of avoiding being imprisoned in any one definition. The root 70.100.2 means heel —and we remember that Jacob is born holding his brother's heel: a clear symbol of this other meaning: "to hold back". The root 70.100.2 stands also for "deceitful, a deep deceit, a provocation", and this meaning obviously has its origin in the biblical narrative. It also stands for "consistent" and "logical", which, after all, is perhaps *Jacob*'s best description.

Genesis xxv, *28-34*. We can now describe the famous meeting of the two brothers. We will not quote the text: *Esau*'s selling his birthright for a mess of pottage is famous in proportion to its absurdity.

The words: *And Isaac loved Esau because he did eat of his venison but Rebekah loved Jacob* (in verse 28) are a key to what follows. We must remember *Rebekah*'s communion with YHWH and therefore her *Yahvic* love for *Jacob*. The text cannot more clearly show a contrast between *Isaac* and *Esau*'s material food and *Rebekah* and *Jacob*'s spiritual nourishment.

Therefore, when we read *Jacob sod pottage* we are bidden to understand those words as symbols. The text (xxv, 29) is: *Ve-Yazed Yaaqov Nazeed*. This is what he does: 6.10.7.4— 50.7.10.4. The 10 and 7 and alternately the 7 and 10 come to a head in the resistance (4) of *Dallet*. We have often insisted on the importance of *Dallet* (the central letter of Adam) as being the backbone of man's resistance to life, and we have seen *Esau*'s deficiency in that respect. The so-called pottage which *Jacob* is said to be cooking is the elaboration of *Israel*'s remarkable perennial striving towards a mature *Adam*.

And Esau came from the field and he was faint. And Yissav said to Yaaqov: Feed me with this Adam, with this very Adam for I am faint: because his name was Edom. Following our previous explanations, this passage is now clear enough when we discard the word pottage which has been arbitrarily added and when we leave the word *Adam* as *Adam*. What *Esau* actually wants, according to the text is: *Min Ha-Adam, Ha-Adam Hazeh*: "of this *Adam*, the *Adam* this one, because his name is *Edom*".

And said *Yaaqov: Mikrah Kayom Et Bekoratekh*. The root *Mikrah* has different meanings and as is generally the case, the tradition has seized upon the wrong one. It can mean "sell", but it also means "to recognize, to know". This is far more correct even grammatically, because there is no "me". The sell "me" is a distortion. "Sell as today" would raise the question "to whom"? And again *Bekoratekh* does not at all mean "your birthright" but "your being the first-born".

So *Yaaqov*'s utterance means: "recognize as today, from beginning to end (*Et*) (or: in its total significance) what is meant by your being the first-born (or your being the early fruit)".

And *Yissav* said: *Behold I am dying. What is it to me to be the (Being) first-born?*

We know that he cannot be hungry or if he is hungry that he can go to his tent and eat the meal that is surely, as usual, prepared for him when he comes from the fields. He is not hungry but *Edom* facing *Adam* is stricken to death. And we remember the conditioned "son of woman" *Abel*, being annihilated by the mere rising of *Cain*-YHWH in front of him. These were the archetypes in the beginning of the myth. But here, where the archetypes are brought down to the level of symbolical human beings, the story is different: *Swear it, said Yaaqov. He swore and acknowledged Yaaqov as elder. And Yaaqov gave Yissav bread and Nazeed Aadasheem and he ate and drank and rose up and did not care who was the elder.*

The schema *Aadasheem* has degenerated into being lentils. In Qabala it is read in several ways. *Aad-Dassa* is symbol of an eternally fructifying vegetation. As to the bread (*Lehhem*) it has been throughout the ages a symbol of communion.

Thus Jacob bestows to his earthly brother the nourishment best fitted to his nature, and this ends one of the most beautiful and most misinterpreted episodes of Genesis.

Esau's acceptance of not being the first-born is necessary to *Jacob*'s incarnation as *Aleph*. It reminds us of *John* 1, *5*: *And the light shineth in darkness and the darkness comprehended it not*. *Esau*'s spiritual submission will allow the myth to be carried by its own impetus towards its symbolical completion. It is to be hoped that when better understood it will hasten towards its actualization.

★

To follow *Jacob* throughout his struggles and adventures would need another book. He seeks safety in flight when *Esau* sets out to kill him, and in exile lends himself as servant to *Laban*. It is a strange, profound and constant unconscious element in history that the *Adams* and the *Edoms*, the dispossessed and the wealthy contend for the colour red. Dressed in purple-red, kings have proclaimed their rights as inheritors of the earth, even as today the disinherited, in pursuit of the same claim, gather around red flags. Red is *Adam*, red is *Edom* and red is the blood.

So goes Jacob, carrying with him nothing more than a blessing. Then we read of his dream, a double ladder where angels descend from heaven to earth and ascend from earth to heaven (symbol of the one living energy) and the appearance of YHWH to him and that place being named *Bayt-El*: house of *Elohim*.

Then *Jacob* in *Hharan*, in the home of *Laban*, son of *Nahhor*; his seven years toil for *Rachel*, and it is *Leah* "whose eyes are weak" that he finds in his bed; and his other seven years for *Rachel* (2 × 7 is a clear symbol); and the servants given to him as wives; and all his children, and his cunning deeds, thanks to which he is able to feed his family and to free himself from *Laban;* and the flight, with *Rachel* riding a camel and sitting on the idols of her father.

Jacob is neither a saint nor a hero. He is no Siegfried, no shining St George fighting dragons. He is *Tam*, simple, hard-

179

working and ingenious enough to gather riches in spite of being exploited and cheated by *Laban*. And when at last he has his freedom, he is old and exhausted.

Genesis XXXII: After having made an agreement with *Laban*, *Yaaqov* is blessed by him. On his return journey, after a whole life in exile, in vision he meets *Elohim*'s angels and he sends messengers to his brother, and he tells them: *Thus shall ye speak unto my lord Esau: Thy servant Jacob saith thus: I have sojourned with Laban and stayed there until now: and I have oxen, and asses, flocks and menservants, and womenservants; and I have sent to tell my Lord, that I may find grace in thy sight.*

The messengers return with the dreadful news that *Esau* is on his way at the head of 400 armed men (note no. 400).

Yaaqov is very much afraid and in distress. He divides his people and his flocks, herds and camels into two camps, thinking that if *Esau* destroys one, the other can perhaps escape, and he prays: *Elohi Ab Avraham Va-Elohi Abi Yitzhhaq. YHWH which saidst unto me: Return into thy country and to thy kindred and I will do thee good! I am too small for all thy mercy and all thy truth which thou hast bestowed upon thy servant and his people. I have passed over the Jordan and now I am become two camps. Deliver me, I pray, from the hand of Esau for I fear him, lest he should come towards me and towards the women and the children; and thou saidst: I will surely do thee good and make thy seed as the sand of the sea, which cannot be numbered (for multitude).*

He settles down for the night in that place and sends to *Esau* a considerable amount of livestock. He then fords a stream with his wives and children. The place is called *Yaboq* (10.2.100). And in great anguish he remains alone in the stillness of the night. Alone and helpless in the dark: what better conditions for *Elohim* to answer his prayer by trying to kill him?

Let us see this clearly: *Yaaqov* is attacked by *Iysh: Aleph-Yod-Sheen*, that is: by the full might of cosmic energy: *Aleph* and *Yod* as the two contradictory aspects of that one energy and *Sheen* as their joint action, *Iysh* is a tremendous concentration of vital energy, and its impact upon *Yaaqov* is a supreme test: the climax

in *Jacob*'s life. If he resists he truly is the carrier of the human
seed.

*And Iysh wrestles with him until the breaking of the day, and sees
that he cannot prevail against him and touches the hollow of his thigh
and the hollow of the thigh is out of joint as he (Iysh) wrestles with him.*

*And he (Iysh) says: Let me go, for the day breaketh. And he (Yaaqov)
says: I will not let thee go except thou bless me. And he (Iysh) says:
What is thy name? And he (Yaaqov) says: Yaaqov. And he (Iysh) says:
not Yaaqov shall be henceforth thy name, but Israel (Yod-Seen-Raysh-
Aleph-Lammed: 10.300.200.1.30) for thou hast fought Elohim and
the generations of men and hast prevailed.*

*And Yaaqov asks and says: Tell me, I pray, thy name. And he (Iysh)
says: Why is it thou ask my name? And he blesses him there.*

*And Yaaqov calls the name of the place Peniel (Pay-Noun-Yod-Aleph-
Lammed: 80.50.10.1.30) because I have seen Elohim face to face and
my breath has been preserved.*

And the sun rises and he passes over Peniel and he is lame.

Genesis XXXIII. Soothed by *Yaaqov*'s most generous gifts and by
his respectful behaviour, *Yissav* kisses him and they both shed
tears, not however before *Yaaqov* had bowed down seven times
and declared *Yissav* as the sun to him.

Following lengthy compliments on both sides, *Esau* invites
Jacob to his place of residence in *Seir*. Answers *Jacob*: *My lord
knows that my children are young and that my flocks cannot go fast. Let
my lord go ahead of me. I will follow him unto Seir.*

Esau therefore goes back to *Seir* and, turning in a different
direction, *Jacob* goes towards *Succot*.

Genesis ends with the story of *Joseph* which has been mentioned in the first part of this book. As to the twelve tribes they
cannot be considered in this volume.

★

Note 1. The question as to whom belongs by right the colour
red appears in *Genesis* XXXVIII, *28-29*: *Tamar*, pregnant by
Judah, has twins. One of them puts out his hand and the mid-

wife binds upon it a scarlet thread. He draws back his hand and the other child emerges. It is interesting to note that that other one is *Pharez,* supposed to be Jesus' ancestor (through his father Joseph).

Note 2. Matthew II, *18,* quoting Jeremiah when relating Herod's tentative murder of the newborn children says: *In Rama was there a voice heard—And weeping and great mourning—Rachel weeping for the children—and would not be comforted—because they are not.*

PART THREE

THE GOSPELS

The Essential Theme

THE ESSENTIAL theme in the myth of Jesus is death and re-surrection. This allegory has been introduced with such pageantry that its protagonist has been deified; the brilliance of the drama has obscured its meaning.

But certain clues, especially in Matthew and John, lead us to understand that the Rabbi who gave rise to his own legend knew quite well the original meaning and the cosmic significance of the *Aleph-Bayt*. In other words, we have every reason to believe that he was a highly initiated Cabalist.

He certainly tried to explain these things to his disciples, but, by their own admission, they did not understand him. We cannot be surprised: Qabala is difficult, even for minds trained in psychology and in philosophy. The churches have either ig-nored it or attempted to refute it (see Hippolytus), or con-demned it when it appeared in what is known as gnosticism (see *Pistis Sophia*).

Jesus—or *Yhshwh* as his name was, according to Qabala—insisted on the essential theme that runs as a visible-invisible thread throughout the Bible: the constant psychological death and resurrection which is the real cosmic call to the human being. Only through that intermittent psychic pulsation of *Aleph* can the creative life manifest itself.

That life is always new. It has therefore neither past nor future. It is not dependent on time or space. It is not "conscious" in the sense we give to that word, because consciousness implies memory. Therefore it is not we who resurrect, but life imper-sonal. And because our thought is always a process of continu-ity in duration, that resurrection is nothing that we can "think".

The process of life eludes our comprehension but we must not allow our intelligence to elude the process of life.

A creed is a system meant to represent that which cannot be represented. It is therefore always a portrayal of images. These images are either, externally, those of beings or objects, or, in the mind, thoughts, intuitions, feelings, sensations.

We can hardly imagine Rabbi *Jesus* resorting to such crude deceptions. It is reasonable to suppose that he was in direct contact with the creative cosmic energies or, in other words, that the Revelation was with him. In that case he could not possibly have conceived a mythology to explain away the mystery that he personified. And it is most improbable that he came to save that which must be destroyed by life, those foci of static, fossilized energy which so often think themselves to be human.

But he did mention the life that can be saved when one "loses" one's life. We will not, however, comment upon his teaching, nor upon the guilt complex that has crystallized around him to the point of relegating him to a far-away heaven and weeping endless tears over his dead body. If we can only explore deeply enough the strange worship of crucified life we can surely discover many of the secret recesses of the human mind.

Hidden behind its unconscious motivations, the psyche, fearful of the unknown, remains dormant in the interpretations of its own myths.

In the next chapters we will deal with two such interpretations: we will see in *Matthew* XVI, *13-25* an episode concerning Peter, and in *John* XIII, 18-*32* the narrative of the Last Supper, which especially concerns *Judas*.

Peter, or Jesus Rejected

MATTHEW XVI, 13-25. In those days Caesarea was a new city. It was founded by Philippi as a result of a Hellenistic revival centred around a miraculous grotto dedicated to the god Pan. The city was built in the Greek style. If the Rabbi *Yhshwh* went there, it was in the hope of introducing his own revival in place of that of an ancient religion which had lost its vitality.

In conformity with the letter-numbers of the original Revelation, the Rabbi designated himself as *Ben-Adam*. The Rabbi affirmed something of great importance. We have only to examine carefully what the letter-numbers of these words convey. First, let us consider *Ben*. The Hebrew letters involved (*Bayt-Noun*) speak to us by means of their numbers (2.700). "Two" means a dwelling, a receptacle. "Seven hundred" means all the possible possibilities open to man (7), raised to the hundreds and thus to cosmic importance. Now, *Adam* (1.4.600, which are the numbers of *Aleph-Dallet-Mem*) gives us, as you may remember, the pulsating, uncreated and creative life within the very blood of man. It is within our capacity either to drown this *Aleph* in our blood or to allow it to resuscitate. (This meaning of *Ben-Adam* as "son of man" evades us.)

Thus *Ben-Adam*, decoded from its numbers, means: "I am the receptacle of everything that can result from the resurrection within me of the living *Aleph*." The Rabbi thus affirms that *Aleph* in its purity springs forth from his own flesh and blood and that his acts are the expression of all that can come forth from *Aleph*, the unknowable, the immeasurable: they do not operate in the world of established structures.

This affirmation places the Rabbi intelligibly as well as intelligently. We can sense his existence at the very heart of the cosmic pulsation: that creative force designated by the *Aleph*, with its letter-number 1. There is no need to graft onto this any anthropomorphic mystery. On the contrary any adjunct whatsoever could only weaken the affirmation made by this integrated man. His affirmation, if properly understood, suffices to destroy all paganism, all idolatries.

In Caesarea, however, it was not understood. And yet the population, little satisfied with the promised "new look" of the old god Pan, was groping for something new. Jesus became the object of this search, as Matthew recorded. When *Yhshwh* asks, *Who do men say that I*, Ben-Adam, *am?* the answer is: *Some say that thou art John the Baptist: some Elias: and others, Jeremiah, or one of the other prophets* (Matt. xvi, 14). It is obvious that no one has understood. Turning then to his disciples, the Rabbi asks, *But who say ye that I am?*

We have only Greek versions of their answer. It is even probable that the first texts of the gospels were in the Hellenistic language. However, certain clues, especially in Matthew, lead us to believe that the Rabbi taught in Hebrew. We can infer from them that Jesus tried to oppose the Hellenistic revival by revealing the deep sense of the original Revelation. But the minds of his contemporaries were not ready to understand the *Aleph-Bayt*.

The Hellenistic answer, attributed to Simon, "Thou art Khristos", is preposterous. The very idea of being called Khristos—or Christ, the Anointed, in modern language—so horrified the Rabbi that he later on *charged . . . his disciples that they should tell no man that he was Jesus Christ* (Matt. xvi, 20). And WHAT HE MEANT COULD NOT HAVE BEEN OTHER THAN WHAT HE SAID.

In Hebrew, Simon probably said: "Thou art *Ben-YHWH-Elohim*" (or *Ben-YHWH*), thus emphasizing the Rabbi's statement. And this answer would have been in accordance with the profound original theme of Genesis, which, ever since the appearance of YHWH, proclaims the primacy of his symbolic

188

offspring over the earth's (*Adamah*'s) offspring of flesh and blood. We remember *Qaheen*, son of this primal cosmic energy, rising above his brother *Hevel*, and *Hevel* thereby being reduced to a mere pool of blood. We have learned, through all the allegories, of the struggle between the *Aleph*, which wills to spring forth, and the blood which tends to stifle it.

In conformity with this process, the Rabbi probably answered Simon in terms of which Matthew still shows some visible signs: *Blessed art thou, Simon Bar-Yona: for flesh and blood hath not revealed it unto thee, but my father which is in heaven* (Matt. xvi, 17).

We know that the "father" is YHWH. As to "heaven", *Shamaim*, we have seen that it is the action of *Sheen* (a cosmic breath) upon the symbolic "waters" (*Maim*) of life as existence, and we also know that it is the action of timeless YHWH permanently pervading the Universe. We can thus compare *Shamaim* and YHWH:

> *Shamaim*: *Sheen-Mem-Yod-Mem*: 300.40.10.40
> YHWH: *Yod-Hay-Waw-Hay*:   10. 5. 6. 5

This comparison of the two schemata reveals that the schema YHWH (as "father") truly is included in *Shamaim*: no. 10 corresponding to 300 shows it in existence, no. 5 and 5 corresponding to 40 and 40 shows them alive, and no. 6 corresponding to no. 10 shows it to be fruitful.

By declaring himself *Ben*-YHWH Jesus identified himself with *Israel*: *And thou shalt say unto Pharaoh, thus saith YHWH, Israel is my son, my first-born* (Exod. iv, 22), and we do not see any reason for not accepting that statement. An interesting fact is Jesus qualifying Simon *Bar-Yona*: son of *Yona*, the dove. It is not generally known that the dove personifying the Holy Spirit has been, since time immemorial, the symbol of Israel.

Let us follow the scene, step by step. *Yhshwh* says, "I am Ben-Adam." Simon must have replied, "I know that you are *Ben*-YHWH." In this reply, the Rabbi sees that Simon understands the origin and ultimate purpose of human evolution.

We do not know to what extent it is possible to unearth a truth buried under centuries of intentional misinterpretations. Apparently it cannot be done by means of exegesis. But the truth included in both Testaments can certainly be discovered when one identifies oneself with the word Israel, whose full meaning is: a continuous and winning battle against *Elohim*. *Israel* is timeless. *Elohim* is temporal.

The Rabbi wishes to establish a human brotherhood. He wishes to condense all human evolution, all duration into one single point. Simon, in a flash of perception, sees that point in the Rabbi because the Rabbi is the transcendence of that which he claims he is. That one single point is the *Aleph* alive, the pulsating timeless life-death-life-death.

Between the Rabbi and Simon, between Simon and the Rabbi a sudden flash of truth explodes, as it will explode for centuries in the minds of millions: it blasts the Hebrew *Yod* and replaces it by *Aleph*.

Yod (10) is the very basis of the religion, as set forth by Moses. This religion knows only the *Yod*: ten males belonging to this religion have the power to perform the authorized religious service. Ten males "unite in heaven" that which they "unite on earth". In a wider sense, the mosaic religion links those who belong to it in an existential, historical *Yod*.

The springing forth of *Aleph* is, on the contrary, a personal event. For a very brief instant Simon, facing Jesus, actually sees *Aleph* in the Rabbi. Seeing it is enough: it is a Revelation. And the Rabbi also sees it in Simon. As soon as it is seen, *Aleph* disappears, slips away because it has, in fact, no existence.

So alas, the second part of the episode is an anticlimax: Simon hears Jesus state the fact: *thou art Ab-ben* (Matt. xvi, 18) *and on Ab-ben I will build.*

The name Peter is derived from the Greek *Petros* which means stone (hence our word "petrify"). It is highly improbable that a Rabbi taught his disciples in Greek. In Hebrew, the word *Aben* (*Aleph-Bayt-Noun*) means stone. According to Qabala "thou art stone", and the building on that petrification conveys the very opposite of what the Rabbi wished to say and do. His essence (the essence of the Hebrew revelation) is life, energy, perpetual movement. In conformity with the cabalistic tradition, Jesus must have used an expression having several different depths of meaning. *Ab-Ben* combines *Ab*: father, and *Ben*: son. It expresses an origin and an end. (It has finally come to serve as name for the philosophers' stone, the supreme object of alchemy, supposed to change base metals into gold.)

Simon, his flash of perception having already passed, and with his limited knowledge and understanding, took upon himself the mission of becoming Peter, thereby of becoming "Satan".

Matthew xvi, 21: *From that time forth began Jesus to shew unto his disciples, how that he must go unto Jerusalem, and suffer many things of the elders and chief priests and scribes, and be killed and be raised again the third day.*

Verse 22: *Then Peter took him, and began to rebuke him, saying, Be it far from thee, Lord: this shall not be unto thee.*

Verse 23: *But he turned, and said unto Peter, Get thee behind me, Satan: thou art an offence unto me: for thou savourest not the things that be of God, but those that be of men.* It is worth noting that this violent condemnation of Peter (in verse 23) follows closely upon verse 19, in which Peter is given *the keys of the kingdom of heaven.*

Satan is a Hebrew word (*Seen-Tayt-Noun*: 300.9.700). In colloquial Hebrew it means the adversary, the accuser, and also Satan, as we know it in English. According to code, we see that the elemental female (9) is held as between pincers by the cosmic breath 300 and the indetermination at stake, 700. It resists both impacts, as it is in its nature to do. Its essence is continuity, its function is proliferation of elementary units.

When *Tayt* prevails it is as a queen-bee or a church, the adversary of the Aleph, of infinite cosmic life-death. In other words *Satan* is a continuity in existence which resists its own necessary destruction. Psychologically, it is a confinement in structures that hinders the flow of life-death in the mind.

The Rabbi was so well aware of this meaning of the word

191

Satan that immediately after having rejected Peter as head of a church, he told his disciples (Matt, XVI, 24-25): *If any man will come after me, let him deny himself and take up his cross and follow me. For whosoever will save his life shall lose it: and whosoever will lose his life for my sake shall find it.*

The rest is a confusion of doubtful symbols that we need not examine: the essential theme of Qabala has made itself apparent in *spite* of . . . *Satan*!

3

Judas, or Jesus Accepted

THE AUTHOR of John's Gospel, whoever he may have been, was familiar with *Aleph-Bayt*. We shall probably never know how any of the Gospels came to be written. It is possible that the original texts were already in the Hellenistic language currently spoken at that time. And perhaps the opening words of John's Gospel, *In the beginning was the Word, and the Word was with God, and the Word was God,* were an attempt to translate *Bereshyt Bara Elohim* for a public who, in any case, could not have understood the ontological meaning of the letter-numbers (or the simple fact that in *Bereshyt* are the elements which create Elohim, and not the reverse). Strangely enough, in their attempt, throughout the centuries, to simplify this difficult language for the understanding of all, the authorities have rendered it incomprehensible. The simpler the text, the less (in this case) its meaning.

In the beginning of this book, it was stated that the composite *Elohim* expresses the life and action of *Aleph*. It was also pointed out that no letter-number—whether *Aleph, Bayt,* or any other—has its full meaning except in its relationship to others. This is because each letter-number is a symbol for one aspect of life's totality. Likewise, every colour in the rainbow is *of* and *in* the light.

In revealing the ontological meanings of the letter-numbers and of their schemata (including *Elohim*) the Qabala permits us to grasp intellectually that which John's Gospel, in any ordinary language, projects under vague symbols.

The original theme developed by John is: *the light shineth in darkness and the darkness comprehended it not* (or received it not)

(John 1, 5). That image can be and *has been* interpreted in a
thousand ways. We feel justified in thinking that that darkness
is the *Hhosheykh*, mentioned in Genesis as opposed to *Awr* (light).
It is the cosmic receptacle of undifferentiated energy which
comes to life when it is fertilized. In the psyche *Hhosheykh* is an
energy that has not yet been structured.

Only when the psyche becomes cognizant of its structured
elements can it die to the perception of itself as continuity. It can
then free itelf from that which appeared as being "contained"
in its sphere of consciousness, but was in fact its "container".
It can open itself to the unutterable reality of *Aleph*. Then, the
marvellous pulsation of life-death can permeate it and the individual is called upon to partake of the universal life.

John the gnostic was cognizant of that truth and he also
knew that it was necessary to strike and wound and trans-
pierce the slumbering minds of his time. He, undoubtedly, was
one of the two disciples who contributed to the enacting of the
tremendous drama of death and resurrection, the other disciple being Judas.

Peter's incomprehension, coming after the lightning flash of
intuition which he had earlier had as Simon, left *Yhshwh* no
hope of making himself understood except by one or two of his
disciples. But how to "stage" so grandiose a symbol? We do
not intend to try to fathom what could have gone on in the mind
of Jesus. We only wish to point to the fact that aside from the
outwardly observed historical events, the collective psyche
pursues its own mythological course. This may well be a determining factor as regards the reality of our world as history
records it. At certain times of great psychological crisis and of
transformation of human consciousness, the collective myth can
even project its images with such violence that they materialize
into all sorts of manifestations, termed occult—such as para-
psychical phenomena, magical apparitions, and mysterious
historical (or hysterical) happenings.

It is likely that such events occurred around the person
called Jesus, whether he really lived during the time of Pontius

Pilate or whether he lived, as many people suppose, about a hundred years previously in the person of a Master of Wisdom among the Essenes. Even taking into account the extravagance of popular imagination concerning his miracles, it is highly probable that this personage did have exceptional powers. These powers, as well as his teachings, have profoundly influenced the human psyche. People find themselves in the impossible situation of "believing" what he taught and at the same time being unable to put these teachings into effect. Who among his believers ceases to worry about tomorrow, either in this world or in the next? Who amongst them relinquishes his possessions, either here or in the hereafter? Or accepts still more blows from an enemy who has already struck him once? Or loves his enemy, etc., etc.? Nothing of all this teaching influences our stubborn desire for self-perpetuation.

Thus, while a great many seek, few find. And from the inner conflict arise our hypocritical morals and all the self-justifications invented by a guilt complex which has been festering for two thousand years. The Rabbi saw that, in his time, the direct comprehension of his teaching was impossible. Thus he was compelled to revert to a symbol.

Whether the characters of this drama actually existed or not is irrelevant: they will live and act in the psyche as long as it is not understood that that myth belongs to mythology.

If the name Judas, burdened with twenty centuries of hatred, is synonym of traitor, it is because it stirs up reactions such as Peter's *This shall not be*, modified after the event into: "Woe, it has been!" and ending in utter confusion. The grief is inconsistent with the facts that the event occurred according to the Father's will; that the will was a sacrifice; that the sacrifice was a redemption; that had it not happened the believers would not have been redeemed from sin; and so on, and so on. . . .

The psyche entangled in its contradictions knows deeply in itself and does not want to know that if "it had not been" life would be peacefully lived in ignorance of its ill-defined culpability.

Of course the psyche does not want to "deny itself" and "lose its life", but craves for continuity. The real culprit, the offender, is none other than Jesus for having stated his necessity as being everyone's necessity. So Jesus is eliminated and sent to an imaginary heaven—and the scapegoat is Judas. As to Peter's church, it rests upon an intricate system of self-preservation originally established in opposition to Jesus' essence: Israel. That was the beginning of theological anti-semitism.

Judas the "traitor" became identified with the "deicides", the Jews. Peter's successors declared themselves to be what they actually were, princes of this world; and the Devil was invented in order to allow the real Satan to operate undisturbed.

These remarks lead us to the deep, vast, sorrowful, cruel drama enacted by mankind. It is difficult to see it in its innermost structure. If it could be thus seen—not only by the few— it would mean a sudden ripening of our state of being.

Let us examine it through John's central symbol: the light, impersonated by Jesus, shines in darkness and the darkness personified by Satan and its princedom (mankind) does not receive it. Obviously, Jesus' purpose is to be received.

Now let us translate this in terms of Qabala: the Rabbi having declared himself *Ben-Adam* is for the time being the personification of the timeless Israel. He is the beginning in the end and the end in the beginning. He does not belong to the time-process. But he wishes to and must "die" in his contact with the historical process, which is of time. He whose name is *YH-Sheen-WH*, that is YHWH in action (Sheen), wants to and must descend deeply into the world (the legend says that he descended so deeply as to go as far as Hell, where he spent three days). By doing so he wishes to and must be in a fleeting duration-non-duration, an actualization of YHWH in the sphere of existence.

The first time, in Caesarea of Philippi he—or the *Aleph* in him—had been recognized but not acknowledged by Peter-Satan. John's Gospel, in the narration of the Last Supper, now shows us, as we read it, that Judas-Satan acknowledged him and obeyed him.

JUDAS, OR JESUS ACCEPTED

The schemata of Jesus and Judas are most revealing:

(Jesus) *Yhshwh*: *Yod-Hay-Sheen-Waw-Hay*: 10.5.300.6.5
(Judas) *Yehouda*: *Yod-Hay-Waw-Dallet-Hay*: 10.5. 6. 4.5

The *Sheen* in YHWH, for Jesus, and the *Dallet* in YHWH, for Judas, are remarkably placed, in inverse order, preceding and following *Waw* (6).

It is to be noticed that Yehoudi in Hebrew means Jew. Its spelling *Yod-Hay-Waw-Dallet-Yod* where the final *Hay* of YHWH is replaced by *Dallet-Yod* means that one of YHWH's *Hay* (life) becomes, with the Jews, an existential resistance to YHWH in *coniuncto oppositorium*, without which YHWH would only be an abstraction.

These oppositions are perfect illustrations of the double contradictory movement so constantly expressed in the Hebrew myth. This movement of life and existence can be compared to a belt that joins two rotating wheels, one above the other. Seen on one side the belt appears to have an ascending motion, seen on the other, it seems to descend. When the movement is very swift, superficial observers do not see it. Thus the revelation appears to them to be fixed, established, by an Abraham, a Moses or a Jesus.

We must now quote the translation of John XIII, 2: *And supper being ended, the devil having now put into the heart of Judas Iscariot Simon's son, to betray him* . . . and we ask: What—or who, in that archaic belief—is the devil?

The origin of this word is to be found in the resistance set by the letter *Dallet*, as we have just seen it (devil, demon, diable, daimon all with a D).

In Jesus-*Yhshwh*, the *Sheen* is a cosmic action. The Hebrew root *Sheen-Dallet* (*Shed*) means violence, ruin, and ultimately, devil. This is one of the many evidences of the forgotten cabalistic origin of the Hebrew language.

The necessary resistance to life, without which life cannot evolve its structures, has become, by the ever-static will of the psyche, a "traitor". In fact, that which gives Judas his impulse is none other than Jesus' Daimon: his active principle.

The Rabbi was very observant of the cabalistic way of thinking. Having identified himself with *Aleph*, he compelled himself to play his part. He knew that *Aleph* is helpless and cannot act, but is acted upon. *Aleph* is buried in *Eretz*, immersed in Adam's blood, murdered when the primordial female prevails, spent when darkness does not "comprehend" it. . . .

Jesus repeatedly, but in vain, tried to have himself arrested. He openly challenged the other rabbis: he attracted enormous crowds; he violated the Sabbath; he raised a scandal in the synagogue; he was socially subversive; and all having been of no avail, he chose to set the Last Supper in the habitual place where he always met his disciples, instead of escaping as he was begged to do.

Are we really supposed to believe that the officers and men did not know that place? That they had not had many better opportunities of arresting Jesus? That they had to be led in the night by Judas? Or course not! Judas and the darkness are more in accord with the myth than with what can have happened, if it ever happened at all.

Jesus has come to fulfil the Scriptures, which means that he must bring them to consummation. They must come to their mythical end. Mythologically, the light (or *Aleph*) is neither accepted by darkness nor can it give itself, and we are to understand that that situation has been in that deadlock ever since the beginning of time.

Any event pertaining to the myth must be perceived in its general context. The one single purpose of the myth is to reveal the possibility of YHWH's penetration into the human race (YHWH being considered in the sense given by the code).

In the beginning *Cain*, personifying "his father" YHWH, annihilated *Abel*, the conditioned man, by his mere presence. Later, in an epic metaphysical poem, the no. 2 of the *Abraham-Isaac-Jacob* triad had to appear in disguise so as to insert what he actually represented (no. 3) into Canaan. He succeeded, but

Esau facing no. 3 (*Jacob*), felt that he was dying. Later still *Jacob* fought during a whole "night" (integrating the total darkness of the mind) to avoid being killed by *Elohim*, but he was wounded by him in *Kaf-Yerekh*: 20.800—10.200.500 (translated: *the socket of his hip*), which means that in his "container" (20) the totality of undifferentiated cosmic energy—or unconscious darkness—(800) came into existence (10) and became cosmically (200) alive (500). Thus wounded, Jacob "limped", the schema being 90.30.70.

That was *Elohim*'s penetration in the body, an event pertaining to evolution in time. Another vital penetration had to occur in the psyche, in the inner life lying in darkness, and that had to transcend time: it had to be YHWH's. But that which is timeless is not in existence in time. It is not in existence: this means that it must die in it. Life must die when plunged into existence.

Jesus came to play the part of *Aleph*. He revealed himself at the symbolic age of 30, was delivered to darkness and acknowledged with the payment of 30 pieces of silver, dying at the age of 33. None of those numbers has any historical foundation, but they are mathematically correct in the myth: Jesus is twice in 30 and dies in twice 3.

We are here in a deep mystery which can be solved as a mathematical equation, but only apprehended through Qabala.

Jesus is the 2nd Person of a Trinity. He is in the same situation as was Isaac: the events are beyond his control, but can they be taken in hand by someone else? Yes and no. The person who will be able to carry on will have to be clearly designated by Jesus (as Jacob was designated by Isaac) and will have to receive his formal investiture.

Isaac had not the power to act but had the power to transfer his power to *Jacob*, and *Jacob* became *Isaac*'s fulfilment.

Likewise, in mathematical cabalistical logic, the Rabbi *Yod-Hay-Sheen-Waw-Hay* had not the power to act but had the power to transfer his power to a chosen disciple, so as to fulfil through him the purpose that the myth had been pursuing *even before the world was* (John XVII, 5).

We have read the story of the Last Supper a thousand times in the four Gospels; and the more we thought about it, the more incomprehensible it seemed. We could not find where or how there was any betrayal in it. *Verily, verily, I say unto you that one of you shall betray me* never rang true; for nothing, either in the beginning or in the end of this narrative, corresponds to what would have happened if a man—or a god—had been betrayed in the execution of his plans. On the contrary, the details of the narrative appeared more absurd in proportion as our conviction grew that they had to do not with an historical fact, but with a psychic reality.

We felt that this narrative was a turning-point in the evolution of the human psyche and that the projection into the narrative of the idea of betrayal was an artifice, *in extremis*, of the psyche, to save itself from any shadow of co-operation in the drama. Here, it was felt was the account of the last game between the two players we had come to know so well: the "mythified" son of heaven and the "mythified" son of earth. And we became convinced that the narrative, whether or not it had been tampered with in the course of the ages by translators, interpreters, priests or *vox populi*, was a libellous record.

Not having the authentic record of this important incident (just where are such accounts to be found?), we could not enquire—as one could in the Book of Genesis—into each letter-number, to discover its true meaning. For no sacred number-language exists in Greek or Latin. The only hope there was of finding a clue lay in the study of other translations to see whether they had been less dishonest than the English version and whether, if so, they could put us on the track of something.

By good luck, the well-known French translation by Louis Segond, Doctor of Theology, gave a clue. Here it is: *En vérité, en vérité, je vous le dis, l'un de vous me livrera* (John XII, 21). The concluding phrase, here, means: One of you will hand me over —or *deliver* me. All of a sudden we had the thrill of discovering

JUDAS, OR JESUS ACCEPTED

something fantastic: the true story of Judas. And the traitor, we saw, is not Judas; the traitor (or rather one of them) is none other than the interpreter who in any one of the false versions has misread the text. As you remember, Jesus is there reported as having said, "One of you shall betray me."

Let us look carefully at the text of John, and notice how the author attempts to make us understand the true picture. If we suppose that Jesus had announced in the presence of the apostles that one of them would be a traitor, what would have happened? Just imagine these men surrounding their beloved Master. Imagine yourself in the situation of the Master telling you, "There is a traitor among us." You, knowing that you were not a traitor, would have jumped to your feet and seized any kind of weapon you could lay your hands on. There would have been eleven of you. And the twelfth would have been quickly overcome and made captive. This is so evident that the very fact of it never having been put forward is just one more proof of how colossal is the psychic barrier, the taboo which humanity has raised against this narrative of Judas for two thousand years. It hardly seems credible, but one must concede that it is so.

John's text is so important that it must be quoted in full.

John XIII, 18-19: *I speak not of you all: I know whom I have chosen: but that the scripture may be fulfilled. He that eateth bread with me hath lifted up his heel against me. Now I tell you before it comes that when it is come to pass ye may believe that I am he.*

In the light of Qabala these verses could hardly be clearer: Jesus is not speaking of all the apostles, but of Judas whom they may think he has chosen by mistake. However, he knows that he has chosen him to fulfil the Scriptures concerning *Ben-Adam.* According to Genesis xxv, 26, the human-to-be seed, *Jacob-Ben-Adam,* was in the womb holding *Esau-Edom*'s heel, lifted against him. Eventually, *Esau*-son-of-the-earth was compelled to confess that *Jacob*-son-of-YHWH was indeed the carrier of the seed, and *Jacob* gave him bread as a token of communion. *Esau* lived, but there was no truce.

However, the fulfilment of the myth and of man must necessarily be an integration in one single individual of the two aspects of vital energy first symbolized by *Cain* and *Abel*, then by *Jacob* and *Esau*, and now by *Jesus* and *Judas*. This is exactly what Jesus says: "now I tell you, before it happens, so that you may believe that I am he". He, meaning obviously Judas if we simply read the text as it is, considering that the "he" mentioned two lines ahead is him.

John xiii, *20-27*. Notwithstanding the clarity of these statements Jesus insists: *Verily, verily I say unto you: He that receiveth whomsoever I send receiveth me, and he that receiveth me receiveth him that sent me.* He will send Judas and Judas will be his *alter ego*.

Then: *When Jesus had thus said he was troubled in spirit.* Why was he troubled in spirit? What could have thus perturbed him? In uttering those words he must have suddenly realized in absolute fact that he, Son-of-YHWH, had actually become incarnate. He had become also son-of-the-earth. It must have been a terrific experience.

We now come to the dramatic *dénouement* and in quoting it I will substitute a more adequate expression for the deadly, the destructive word, "betray".

... *and (Jesus) testified, and said, Verily, verily, I say unto you, that one of you shall* HAND ME OVER (OR, DELIVER ME). *Then the disciples looked one on another, doubting of whom he spake. Now there was leaning on Jesus' bosom one of his disciples whom Jesus loved. Simon-Peter therefore beckoned to him, that he should ask who it should be of whom he spake. He then lying on Jesus' breast saith unto him, Lord, who is it? Jesus answered, He it is, to whom I shall give a sop, when I have dipped it. And when he had dipped the sop, he gave it to Judas Iscariot, the son of Simon. And after the sop Satan entered into him. Then said Jesus unto him, That thou doest, do quickly.*

Here again the text is so clear that it cannot be misunderstood if we do not interpret it wilfully in such fashion as to infer from it the opposite of what it says.

In spite of two thousand years of theology, the only one with whom Jesus communes is Judas, and however bewildering for the minds that can only function one way, the direct effect of that communion is that Jesus introduces Satan into Judas.

And now, having materialized Satan, Jesus speaks to him as a master to his dependant: *That thou doest, do quickly!*

John XIII, *28-30: Now no man at the table knew with what intent he spake unto him. For some of them thought, because Judas had the purse, that Jesus had said unto him, Buy those things that we have need of against the feast; or that he should give something to the poor. He then having received the sop went immediately out: and it was night.*

None of the eleven were aware of what was happening. We know that they were half asleep, or mesmerized, or probably overwhelmed by the tremendous outpouring of energy that was to shatter forever the foundations of the human mind.

The most decisive words of any myth in any time had been uttered. And now had come the moment of suspense.

And those words, for some of those men, so deeply slumbering, have meant "go and buy cakes" . . . Moreover it was night: what a time for such errands!

But John is now aware. He, so near his Master, as actually to be touching him, must feel the tremendous vibrations. What is it that he sees? How does he know? Many years later when dictating his Gospel to his disciples, he stated that *Satan* entered into *Judas*. Was it a conclusion? A knowledge acquired at the end of his life?

We cannot answer these questions, and they are not relevant. Our real question is: this suspense is not of time, therefore it is now, here, facing us and in us. Do we see it? Do we feel it? Do we understand it?

Here are, in us, standing face to face, Jesus and *Judas*. Who are they? What are they? And we hear Jesus giving his order: What you are to do, do it quickly, and John has just told us that this order is given to Satan who has taken possession of Judas.

Have we emptied our minds of all the infantile ideas and pictures of the "devil"? Have we deeply integrated every myth and mythology? Are we actually inside the inexplicable mystery of all that exists? If so, we can understand and rejoice: *John* XIII, *31-32*.

Therefore when he was gone out, Jesus said Now is the son of man glorified and God is glorified in him. If God be glorified in him, God shall also glorify him in himself and shall straightway glorify him.

We can no longer be deterred by the real meaning expressed in such a symbolic and archaic way: the fact has been stated already: he that receives the one that Jesus sends receives Jesus and receives the one that sent Jesus. It is clear that Jesus sends Satan. So he who receives Satan receives Jesus, hence he receives God.

In terms of traditional religion this statement, in spite of it being so clearly written in John's Gospel is monstrous and frightening.

In terms of gnosis it is the statement of a simple fact: there is only One energy, only One life, only One movement. All is one and one is in all. The One is the one game of life and existence, of energy as energy and of energy as its own physical support, which is its own resistance to itself, without which nothing would be.

4

Epilogue

THIS NARRATIVE has neither beginning nor end. It has to do with the drama of the human mind, enclosed in its psychical egg shell. It deals with the tragedy of timeless life imprisoned therein, life which more often than not is extinguished by the hardening of the shell.

We have tried to elucidate what the unfortunate Hellenization of the ancient Hebrew Revelation has termed Logos or Word. The entire Revelation is contained in the meaning of *Aleph, Bayt, Ghimel, Dallet,* and the rest of the letter-numbers of the sacred language. Far more than a mere series of letters, they represent an anatomy of the cosmic interplay of energies and resistances of which each of us is but a transient condensation. Now the Door is opened, or rather we have a key to it. For the time being, let us go no further. Anyone who so desires can move into the vitalizing study and dig—not too long in the Book itself, but in his own mind, going on indefinitely making his own discoveries.

It is possible to bring down the working of the cosmic principles, so to speak, to a point where we can see them functioning in our daily life. Thus it is in our everyday behaviour and in the working of our mind that Genesis and Yhshwh's teachings can be fruitful. We can be a point of consciousness to which the Revelation comes. But this we cannot be if we cling to traditional belief, ritual and authority founded upon the misunderstanding and negation of the essential truths of these teachings. All such philosophies, theologies, creeds or worship—whether spiritualistic or materialistic, individual or social—are but static projections of the psyche: of a shell.

The potential effect of the "Word", as we perceive it through the living significance of *Aleph-Bayt*, is not just a sterile reaction against organized religions that have grown around it. On the contrary, meeting the tremendous challenge of this re-reading can be as fruitful as the emergence of a germ of life when, at its proper stage of maturity, it shatters the shell that encloses it. The protection afforded by its dwelling, the *Bayt*, is necessary during growth; but carried into maturity, it suffocates the *Aleph* within.

Once more let it be emphasized that what we have tried to convey in this book has to do with the germ, the inner core of humanity as seen from within, from the very essence of it. Our time calls for maturity. This is what we are called upon to attain. We need but to stand receptive in the way of the blessing of maturation, which is the breaking of the shell that bars us from interaction with the universal life-force.

Human history has been the record of a monstrous massacre. For centuries it has recounted stories of wholesale slaughter in wars, decapitations, mutilations, and death by fire and torture. Our epoch, far from eliminating these barbarities, girds itself for even more monstrous destruction with computers for "perfecting" the means to this end. No less brutal is the fact that the greater part of humanity suffers from poverty, ill health and hunger.

Considering the appalling martyrdom of hundreds of millions of human beings, it is strange that one single death, unrecorded in its time and hence of uncertain occurrence—the death of Jesus on the cross—has generally assumed such magnitude in human consciousness as to overshadow virtually all the others. The reason lies in the fact that the psyche lives its own history in parallel with recorded history. Psychological events, being lived directly, are often far more stirring than concrete facts. There is no better illustration of this than the Crucifixion itself, casting as it does its tremendous shadow over the world.

The psyche may not be aware of the historical conditions which, at the time of Pontius Pilate, transformed the pleasant

Hellenistic mythology into a tragedy. The symbols typified by Zeus and his half-heavenly, half-human offspring were shifted to a new aspect of the pagan Father and his son, thus obliterating the Hebrew revelation and all that the Rabbi Yhshwh did and said according to that ancient tradition. Therefore, his teaching of love has persisted in the realm of the thoughts of men—which are "of Satan"—and has been disconnected from the source, which is timeless, ever fresh and new, beyond all measure and transcending all thought.

The Light that was Crucified

THROUGHOUT THIS essay, from Adam to Jesus, we have introduced vibrations that should, up to a point, help certain
psyches to overcome a passive stage of development that fixes
them as chrysalids in a condition in which they are in danger
of dying whilst dreaming their myths.

For fear of facing the uncertainties of real space, these psyches
wither in imaginary celestial regions, all the more deceptive in
that they are linked to historical events.

The reversing of values, thanks to which the psyche anaes-
thetizes itself, transforms at all costs a myth into an historical
reality whose existence is violently denied by those who believe in
a contradictory myth. These opposing views sometimes lead to
the most fantastic inventions, as for example, the narrative
linked to the talmudic tradition called *Toledot Yeschou*, in which
Jesus is said to have been the illegitimate son of a woman hair-
dresser and of a certain *Pandera*.

The passionate arguments between the early Church Fathers
and the Rabbis concerning the origins of their respective revelations have unfortunately engulfed the fundamental religious
problem in a morass of historical interpretations. The opposing
parties pursued their arguments with fierce tenacity on sub-
jects such as the crossing of the Red Sea by the Hebrews, or
the question of who were the witnesses of Jesus' empty sepulchre.
It was of prime importance to them that things should have
happened in a certain way and not otherwise.

Such discussions about Moses, Jesus or the Buddha have
always been and still are based upon a dualistic conception:
the existence of two different worlds (this one and the one

above or beyond) and upon the idea that one or other of the exalted founders of these religions has opened a line of communication between this world and the other. The resulting creeds are therefore based upon ritual, prayers and other forms of worship that are claimed to lead to the unknown.

The essential point of each creed is to prove that its founder has actually opened the said line of communication. The evidences brought forth are usually miracles, apparitions, voices calling, meteorological phenomena, which infer that to prove its existence the other world must upset this one.

We have often said that the primary purpose of all established religions is to prevent, to remove from the mind, the perception of the immediate all-pervading mystery: the fact that the mere existence of anything at all cannot and never will be explained.

We think that justice has been done to Moses in ignoring his miracles and in stating that his religion was the building of a protective shell for a profound truth: a shell that has no longer any purpose.

Likewise, we must do justice to Jesus in eliminating his miraculous aspects that have nothing to do with the truth which can be discovered in the original Hebraic myth: the game of indetermination played by *Aleph* and *Yod*.

When that game is truly perceived by us, YHWH springs alive and the *spirit of truth* (*John* xiv, *16-17*), foretold by Jesus, dwells within us.

The important point of contact between Hebraism and early Christianity can only be shown in the almost unknown link between the original Qabala and Gnosticism, against which the Church built its defences. We will point out some of its elements, without which this essay would not be complete.

According to *Matthew* xxviii, Mary Magdalene and the other Mary go to the sepulchre, there is an earthquake, an angel descends from heaven like a bolt of lightning, the keepers almost die of fright, the angel says that Jesus has been resurrected, the women depart, Jesus meets them, they fall at his feet and worship him. Later on, the disciples (except *Judas*) see Jesus on a mountain in Galilee, they worship him *but some doubted*.

According to *Mark* xvi, Mary Magdalene, Mary the mother of James and Salome go to the sepulchre, they see there a stone that has been rolled away and a young man dressed in white; they are very much afraid, the young man tells them to notify *his disciples and Peter* (note the obvious interpolation). They run away. *After that he appeared in another form unto two* disciples. He later appeared to the eleven and then *he was received into Heaven and sat on the right hand of the Lord.* (Note this last mythological touch, coming straight from Olympus.)

According to *Luke* xxiv unnamed women go to the sepulchre with spices, two men are standing there *in shining garments*; they say that Jesus has risen according to his promise. That same day two disciples, one of them named *Cleophas* and the other unnamed are on the road to *Emmaus*. Jesus meets them on the way, *but their eyes were holden that they should not know him.* They walk and spend the whole day together, Jesus speaking at length. In the evening *their eyes were opened and they knew him and he vanished from their sight. And they said one to another: Did not our heart burn within us while he talked with us by the way, and while he made plain to us the scriptures?*

According to *John* xx, Mary Magdalene alone goes to the sepulchre, sees it empty, runs and tells Peter and John. The two go with her to the sepulchre and see the linen shroud lying on the floor. Mary weeps and sees *two angels in white, sitting.* They ask: why do you weep? She says: *because they have taken away my Lord* . . . Then . . . *she turned and saw Jesus standing and knew not that it was Jesus* (v. 14). He speaks to her but she *supposes him to be the gardener* (v. 15). Then he calls her "Mary" and she says *Rabboni, which is to say Master* (v. 16), but he tells her not to touch him.

That same day Jesus appears to the disciples *when the doors were shut* (v. 19). Having thus appeared, he shows his hands and his side so as to be recognized, and speaks briefly to them. Thomas is not there. When the others tell him about the appearance, he does not believe them. He says that unless he touches Jesus he will not believe that he came in the flesh. Eight days later the disciples are again together, Thomas included. Jesus appears again, *the doors being shut* (v. 26). He tells Thomas to reach out his hand and to touch him, and adds: *be not faithless but believing* (v. 27) and Thomas believes *without touching him.*

The strangest narration concerning these apparitions is in *John* xxi.

Seven disciples are on the shore of Lake Tiberias. Simon-Peter says: *I go a-fishing. They say unto him, we also go with thee.* That night they do not catch anything. *But when the morning was now come, Jesus stood on the shore: but the disciples knew not that it was Jesus.* He tells them to *cast the net on the right side of the ship* and they cannot draw it in because it is so full of fish. Then John says: *it is the Lord* and Simon-Peter who was naked puts on his coat and plunges into the lake(!) The others come in a little boat, dragging the net full of fish.

When the discrepancies are eliminated from all these narratives, the constant factors are the presence of Mary Magdalene, the absence of Mary the mother, and above all the fact that when Jesus appears he is not recognized and that when eventually he is recognized, he does not allow anybody to touch him.

According to *Matthew*, some of the disciples "doubt". According to *Mark*, he appears "in another form". *Luke* resorts to an euphemism: "their eyes were holden that they could not see", but he finally states that after a whole day Jesus is at last recognized because of what he said, which is a most strange way of recognizing a person with whom one has lived until three days before that particular meeting.

John the Gnostic is the clearest of all. He knows that the most successful way to hide a secret is to say it openly but casually. It was very astonishing when it was discovered that, in the narration concerning Thomas, Jesus appears when the doors are shut. In relating this story John carefully repeated that statement for fear that it should be overlooked. When the form of Jesus appears the second time and meets Thomas, Thomas is persuaded that faith is better than knowledge. Once before it did not allow Mary Magdalene to touch it.

Concerning the apparition on the shore of Tiberias, John quotes himself as having said: It is the Lord, when he was told where the fish were: poor evidence indeed. Simon-Peter's behaviour is farcical as the story goes, but not in symbol; he puts on his coat and jumps into the lake, instead of meeting his Master on the shore.

This passage and the following concerning Peter were written in order to be understood by cabalists and gnostics. Their meaning was eventually lost. It is not our purpose to examine them in detail, but it must be shown in which direction one must look.

Simon-Peter puts on his coat and does not forget to tighten his belt (*he girt his fisher's coat*, says the text); he then goes into the water. This is exactly the opposite of what is known to be the ritual of certain initiations. We recall Joseph being stripped naked by his brothers and thrown into a dry well, and we said that the episode is the distorted narrative of a ceremony of initiation. John, for those who know how to read, says that Peter is in a regressive stage. His further dialogue with the form of Jesus is revealing. Jesus would never have offered his love to the highest bidder: in verses 15, 16 and 17 the apparition asks three times of the man who had three times denied Jesus if he loves it more than the others do. Peter says he does. Then three times it says: *Feed my sheep*.

These words, according to Qabala, are the best evidence that this apparition behaved as *Satan*, because to be the sheep of anyone, even the sheep of Almighty God, if such a being exists, is an abomination to *Ben-Adam*.

In brief, when all those narratives concerning the resurrection are considered, there can be no doubt as to the correct view of docetism concerning it. According to that early doctrine, Jesus never appeared in the flesh, but in an "astral" body, as theosophists would call it today. The apparitions were not denied by docetism, nor do we see any reason not to consider

THE LIGHT THAT WAS CRUCIFIED

them as metapsychical phenomena such as have often been observed and studied.

The early fathers of the Church fiercely refuted docetism but with very unconvincing arguments, except where simple faith in resurrection of the flesh is called for. Our contention, however, is that the entire question is irrelevant and immaterial. It only detracts from the essential, which is our psychical maturity and our impregnation by cosmic energies capable of recreating us anew from moment to moment.

One of the most important Gnostic archetypes is Mary Magdalene. Of its many names we will only mention *Myriam M'Gadola*. The root *Mareh* (*Mem-Raysh-Aleph-Hay*) in Hebrew means image, appearance, vision, mirror (whence derives the English word: mirror). *Iam* is always a reference, to the sea or to a still water acting as a mirror. *G'dola* means big.

The Mary Magdalene out of whom Jesus *had cast seven devils* (*Mark* xvi, 9) is the female element transfigured by this "casting out" of no. 7. This archetype is visionary in a real sense; it is, in its symbolical form, the woman exorcized by her cosmic spouse and sanctified by the expulsion of the seven resistances to the sacred no. 7 of indetermination. She is the necessary witness, the only possible witness to the resurrection of *Aleph*. She is the eternal prostitute, eternally redeemed and regenerated: the human psyche. Mary Magdalene is symbolically—and alas only symbolically—the final act of a drama that the mind dreams for fear of losing itself in its completion.

With *Myriam M'Gadola* or Magdalene we are at the very centre of the essential elements of the myth, in the deepest symbols of Qabala, of Gnosis, of alchemy, and of many other expressions of what is often included in the words "occult" or "esoteric".

As we read this schema we see it to be similar to a peaceful mirror of still waters. It reflects the vision that the living light projects upon the world. It is the vision that the world projects upon the world. It is the vision that the world projects upon light. It is the substance purified: the structured energy as it appears to itself in its own evolution. It is the perpetual gnostic throbbing of energy in a symbiosis of pregnancy and virginity.

Myriam M'Gadola emerges from the vast primordial mass of waters, from the perpetual undifferentiated energy constantly expanding in its apparent evolution. Energy, in spite of building its own container, cannot resist itself to the point of containing itself.

Through the entire myth we have now seen how energy is structured, from the undifferentiated stage to the indeterminate stage, by the interplay of the four symbolical elements.

Water mixed with earth must pass through fire's formative power to gather resistance, and air is the transmitting element. Those elements are primitive and archaic for the non-initiate, who only consider them in their objective reality, but in truth it is very difficult to follow them symbolically and psychologically through the evolution of the myth.

Fire and Air are male. Earth and Water are female. Light (*Awr*) is, as we have seen, the copulation of *Aleph* represented by Fire and Air and of its cosmic container, *Raysh* represented by Earth and Water. The results of their union is an evolution of the Female: inorganic exterior light becomes organic and inner, through a process of differentiation which culminates (for our planet) in man.

One of the aspects of this myth is the birth of a deity and the virginity of its mother. This theme is far from being specifically Christian: it existed in many ancient civilizations. When it is taken literally and considered to be an historical event the belief in that objectivity is a subjective matter. The stronger the objectivity, the deeper the subjectivity: the psyche seeks in it a refuge, a fixation, and thereby stifles the *Aleph* and its eternal life.

It may well be that the greatest error of the Christian dogma is the assertion that the Holy Ghost engendered an infant only once, and at a certain date. It is irrational to think that the timeless, unthinkable, infinite immanence is not in all times and in all places in intimate copulation (symbolically speaking) with the world since it constantly bears fresh and unexpected fruits.

The real feminine archetype in this myth is the perpetual lover, Mary Magdalene, and not Mary-Mother-of-Jesus who belongs to the past and is therefore in a state of regression. When the archetypes are thus understood, the fact that Jesus rejects his mother, and repeatedly refuses her advances, far from appearing strange and abnormal strikes us as being in perfect accordance with the myth.

Having identified Myriam as the psyche we can understand how the human mind, when it is really in love with the infinite cosmic energy, can always be impregnated by it, thereby becoming perpetually fresh, new, virgin. It may give its fruit but it never is its "mother". It can progress on the path of understanding so far as to emit the spark of *Aleph*. The spark dies and resurrects intermittently and does not acknowledge its mother.

We are never justified in approaching the problem of knowledge by reversing its symbols. These images are but projections of the individual and the collective unconscious. They are regressive, they belong to the past, whereas knowledge is the immediacy of our own maturity.

The crucifixion then, assumes its proper meaning: far from being a torture and a death it appears to be a relaxation, a rest: it is both the separation and the union of the invisible *Aleph* and of the material *Yod*. It is a life so intense as to appear motionless, its vibration being too swift to be perceived.

The real cross is alive. It is nowhere as clearly depicted as in the shape of *Aleph*. Its diagonal line expresses the primordial element of life, and I believe that biologists have indeed discovered that organic life begins when an element in crystallization is thus set. On the upper right hand side of *Aleph* a sign in the shape of a hammer suggests the hammering of the invisible world, and on the lower left hand side a sign in the shape of a leg suggests the march of time.

However eloquent, that figure is only a symbol. We must

never forget that any description of *Aleph* fails to describe it: *Aleph* transcends thought. This assertion is fundamental in Qabala and in Gnosticism.

Cabalists, it can be said, in brief, explored the structure of energy, outer and inner. Gnostics have emphasized the inner life. Both have rejected the canonical teaching according to which the inner life can be lived vicariously by means of an objectified myth.

According to Gnosis, therefore, the crucifixion exists and yet does not exist; it happened and yet it did not happen; it is of time and yet it is not in the process of time.

As an example of those mystic texts, here is a quotation from part of the Gnostic Acts, known as the Leucian Acts of John, taken from an English translation of this by G. R. S. Mead, published as far back as 1907.* They purport to date from very early times, before the Gnostics came to be considered heretical, that is to say prior to A.D. 150—say about A.D. 130. To our mind, it is enough that such things have been thought and lived. In the myth, which is the true history of the psyche, there is greater revelation of truth than in any chronicle of the time. These inspired writings deserve to be widely known.

The first of the passages which we wish to quote from these Acts of John is a Mystery Play, danced and sung by Jesus, whilst his disciples move in a circle around him, responding with "Amen" at the end of each verse:

We praise thee, O Father;
We give thanks to thee, O Light;
In whom darkness dwells not.

. . . . . .

I would be saved and I would save
I would be loosed and I would loose
I would be wounded and I would wound
I would be dissolved and I would dissolve
I would be begotten and I would beget

* *The Hymn of Jesus* and *The Gnostic Crucifixion* (Stuart & Watkins).

I would eat and I would be eaten
I would hear and I would be heard
I would understand and I would be all understanding
. . . . . .
I would flee and I would stay
. . . . . .
I would be atoned and I would atone
I have no dwelling and I have dwellings
I have no place and I have places
I have no temple and I have temples
I am a lamp to thee who seest me
I am a mirror to thee who understandest me
I am a door to thee who knockest at me
I am a way to thee a wayfarer.
. . . . . .

Now, answer to my dancing. See thyself in me who speak and seeing what I do, keep silence on my mysteries.

Understand by dancing what I do, for thine is the Passion of man that I am to suffer.

Thou couldst not at all be conscious of what thou dost suffer were I not sent as thy word by the Father.

Seeing what I suffer, thou sawest me as suffering; and seeing, thou didst not stand, but wast moved wholly, moved to be wise.

Thou hast me for a couch: rest thou upon me; but who I am thou shalt not know when I depart; what now I am seen to be, that I am not. But what I am thou shalt see when thou comest.

If thou hadst known how to suffer, thou wouldst have power not to suffer. Know then how to suffer and thou hast power not to suffer.
. . . . . .

As for me, if thou wouldst know what I was: in a word, I am the Word who did dance all things . . .

'Twas I who leapt and danced.

(And here John himself takes up the narrative.)

(1) And having danced these things with us, Beloved, the

217

Lord went out. And we, as though beside ourselves, or wakened out of sleep, fled each our several ways.

(2) I, however, though I saw the beginning of his passion could not stay to the end, but fled to the Mount of Olives, weeping over that which had befallen.

(3) And when he was hung on the tree of the cross, at the sixth hour of the day, darkness came over the whole earth. And my Lord stood in the midst of the cave, and filled it with light and said:

(4) John! To the multitude below in Jerusalem, (it appears that) I am being crucified and pierced with spears; and reeds and vinegar and gall are being given to me to drink. To thee now I speak, and give ear to what I say, 'Twas I who put it in thy heart to ascend this mount, that thou mightest hear what a disciple should learn from master and man from God.

(5) And having thus spoken he showed me a cross of light set up, and around the cross a vast multitude, and therein one form and a similar appearance, and in the cross another multitude not having form.

(6) And I beheld the Lord Himself above the cross. He had, however, no shape, but only as it were a voice—not, however, this voice to which we were accustomed, but one of its own kind and beneficent and truly of God—saying unto me:

(7) John, one there needst must be to hear these things from me; for I long for one who will hear.

(8) This cross of light is called by me for your sake sometimes Mind, sometimes Jesus, sometimes Christ, sometimes Door, sometimes Way, sometimes Bread, sometimes Seed, sometimes Resurrection, sometimes Son, sometimes Father, sometimes Spirit, sometimes Life, sometimes Truth, sometimes Faith, sometimes Grace.

(9) Now, those things it is called as towards men; but as to what it is, in truth, itself, in its own meaning to itself and declared unto us, it is the defining and limitation of all things, both the firm necessity of things fixed from things unstable and the harmony of wisdom.

(10) And as it is wisdom in harmony, there are those on the right and those on the left—powers, authorities, principalities and daemons, energies, threats, powers of wrath, slandering— and the lower Root from which have come forth the things in Genesis.

(11) This then is the Cross which by the Word has been the means of "cross-beaming" all things, at the same time separating off the things that proceed from Genesis and those below it, from those above, and also compacting them all into one.

(12) But this is not the cross of wood which thou shalt see when thou descendest hence; nor am I here that is upon the cross, I whom now thou seest not, but only hearest a voice.

(13) I was held to be what I am not, not being what I was to many others; nay, they will call me something else, abject and not worthy of me. As, then, the place of rest is neither seen nor spoken of, much more shall I, the Lord of it, be neither seen nor spoken of.

(14) Now, the multitude of one appearance round the cross is the lower nature. And as to those whom thou seest on the cross, if they have not also one form, it is because the whole race of him who descended hath not yet been gathered together.

(15) But when the upper nature, yea, the race that is coming unto me in obedience to my voice, is taken up, then thou who now harkenest to me, shalt become it, and it shall no longer be what it is now, but above them, as I am now.

(16) For so long as thou callest not thyself mine, I am not what I am. But if thou harkenest unto me, hearing, thou too shalt be as I am, and I shall be what I am when thou art with thyself, as I am with myself; for from this, thou art.

(17) Pay no attention, then, to the many; and them that are without the mystery, think little of: for know that I am wholly with the Father and the Father with me.

(18) Nothing, then, of the things which they will say of me have I suffered; nay, that Passion as well, which I showed unto thee and the rest by dancing it, I will that it be called a mystery.

THE CIPHER OF GENESIS

(19) What thou art, thou seest; this did I show unto thee. But what I am, this I alone know, and no one else.

(20) What then is mine, suffer me to keep; but what is thine, see thou through me. To see me as I really am I said is not possible, but only what thou art able to recognize as being kin to me.

(21) Thou hearest that I suffer, yet I did not suffer; that I suffered not, yet I did suffer; that I was pierced, yet I was not smitten; that I was hanged, yet I was not hanged; that blood flowed from me, yet it did not flow; and in a word, the things they say about me I had not, and the things they do not say, those I suffered. Now what they are I will riddle for thee; for I know that thou wilt understand.

(22) Understand, therefore, in me, the slaying of a Verb, the piercing of a Verb, the blood of a Verb, the hanging of a Verb, the passion of a Verb, the nailing of a Verb, the death of a Verb.

(23) And thus I speak, separating off the man. First, then, understand the Verb, then shalt thou understand the Lord and in the third place only, the man and what he suffered.

(24) And having said these things to me and others, which I know not how to say as he himself would have it, he was taken up, no one of the multitude beholding him.

(25) And when I descended I laughed at them all, when they told me what they did concerning him, firmly possessed in myself of this only, that the Lord contrived all things symbolically and according to dispensation for the conversion and salvation of man.

Circumcision

WE BELIEVE that circumcision is an important factor in the Genesis of man (or resurrection of *Aleph*). We therefore offer here a tentative introduction to the study of its physiological and psychological consequences.

The foreskin, in enveloping the gland, shelters it from all contact. Because of this protection the non-circumcised child lives until the age of puberty as if that organ, as a sexual organ, did not exist—except in those momentary states of excitation to which, as everyone knows, the child is subject. At such times the mucous lining, which is very sensitive, causes a strongly localized pleasure in the sexual organ. It is not until puberty that the gland undergoes exterior contacts sufficient to establish an active transmission throughout the whole sexual system. Until that time, the system can be compared to a dead-end street, without traffic, without exchange, inasmuch as the fixation of the centre of interest is blocked at the entrance.

The practice of circumcision on the young child results in (1) a physiological shock, accompanied by (2) a partial desensitizing of the gland (which makes, later on, for a lack of violently concentrated sensation) and followed by (3) an indefinite prolongation of the sexual shock in the whole organism because of the uncovering of the gland. From that time on, the gland will continually undergo contacts which will be transmitted to nerve centres, to an entire apparatus still in the original stage and incapable of any impulse towards sexual functioning. We know that the sexual instrument is not isolated. It is in contact with the sensorial functioning of all the senses. (This is evident when an erotic state transforms the five senses, conferring upon them an erotic character and focusing them for its own use.)

This awakening in the child obviously cannot bring forth in him capacities which he does not possess. However, with equal opportunity, his faculties will be better organized and exploited.

This is not the only aspect of the question, nor is it, perhaps, the most important. Circumcision in the extremely young child creates a shock around which the psyche builds itself. It is true that an important shock has already taken place: the birth trauma, recorded in the crystallization of a "snowball" of reactions which will become the self. But the trauma of circumcision immediately introduces within that psyche a mobile element; it is not buried as soon as it is produced, but is prolonged indefinitely and radiates within the vital centres during their formative periods.

Thus, in the non-circumcised, the psyche is crystallized around a birth trauma, which is slowly but surely interred by the child's reactions to his environment. The younger the child, the more malleable he is, so that these reactions act upon him like a mold.

This procedure is violently troubled by circumcision at eight days, because it introduces a purely individual shock, a moving traumatism that concerns the very fibres of his being. Instead of a slow condensation of fluctuating elements determined by the surroundings, we find an active, awakened, vital centre in full process of organization, capable of transforming its reactions to the environment into purely individual elements. Not only does the individual consciousness—the "I"—construct itself more rapidly, but its foundations are laid in a living, flexible element constantly related to the development of the individual.

But how is a woman affected by all this? And is the social attitude of the Jew influenced by circumcision? The Jewish woman is, indeed, transformed by the fact of the man's having been circumcised. This practice, having existed for many centuries, has brought about certain hereditary modifications in both male and female: these include a great nervous sensibility due to an especially complex nervous system, always on the *qui vive*, always mobile and on the watch, ready to shift balance, even to lose balance; a precocious, sometimes excessive intellectuality; and a mind which, though strongly determined, is nevertheless mobile and pliable.

Besides the hereditary transmission of qualities such as these, there exists a Jewish mode of behaviour, on the part of man which necessarily reacts upon woman, and also a particular state of consciousness that expresses itself socially. (It is dangerous to venture into generalizations. Besides, "the circumcision of the hearts" which was mentioned some two thousand years ago, would be, if understood, the quickest and most revolutionary way towards human fulfilment.)

Sex is obviously a determining factor in every society. Being a projection of cosmic energies, it can well be translated in terms of *Aleph* versus *Yod*. At the bottom of the scale, in one of the most primitive manifestations, we see the male bee dying in the sexual act. In such societies, the female organizes an immutable functional order, in which the *Aleph* is constantly murdered. On a higher animal level, the sexual activity is dependent on recurrent needs, and both males and females are conditioned by seasonal rhythms. The species cannot evolve; they remain within the framework of *Tov*, which is continuity in time.

The human condition is a state of conflict, a struggle, symbolically between YHWH, who aims at freeing the *Aleph*, and Eretz (the earth) who, as we have seen, "drinks the blood" of Hevel, his Adam bereaved of *Aleph* (dam meaning blood).

Let us now consider the three following cases: (*a*) non-circumcision; (*b*) circumcision at puberty: that of Ishmael, son of Hagar, the enslaved woman; (*c*) circumcision at eight days: that of Isaac, son of Sarah.

The uncircumcised. For the uncircumcised, the eruption at puberty of a centrifugal force generally leads to an upheaval. At that age, a deep sexual disturbance may be felt by an unprepared organism. New, unexpected sensations upset the static balance prevailing hitherto (or, alas, not upsetting it, leave it static). An outburst takes place, as after the bursting of a dam. Naturally, these cases are extreme; and once again, one cannot generalize, for one can easily find cases of sexual development which invalidate these remarks in one way or another. But one thing is certain: cases of sexual "revelation", of disturbance of masculine vitality, of interior realization, or of reorganization of spiritual life due to coitus, are not the case of Israel. It is equally certain that the search for union by identification of two beings in the sexual act and the desire to plunge into the sexual abyss in order to be identified with the great "vital currents" of nature (as sung or described by writers and vaunted as being the source of spiritual, artistic and passionate ideals) are an abomination in the eyes of Israel, circumcised at eight days and carrying in his flesh the pact with Elohim.

Circumcision at puberty. Quite different is the result of circumcision when it takes place at the age of thirteen (the boy's age of puberty), as is the case among followers of the Moslem faith. With the violent sexual shock, at the prodrome of puberty, the sensorial perceptions suddenly become purely sexual. This drains the masculine energy towards sex, maintaining it there in a continually erotic state. As a consequence of this practice, a stoppage of the intellectual faculties and even a regression due to sexual excess may be produced.

Circumcision at eight days. A manner of confronting the paradoxical double movement of which we are made is presented by circumcision at eight days (*Aleph* versus *Yod*). It not only polarizes the subconscious around an awakening vital energy and constructs within a mobile psyche, but the contributary elements are, themselves, mobile.

When, at the age of two or three months, the intelligent coordination of movement begins to occur, there is already, in the circumcised child, a subconscious "nucleus" around the sensorial activity which engendered it. The psychophysical exchanges become intense. The young self, attached to its vital centres, gradually eliminates the elements imposed by its environment, and, because of this, finds itself carried away by a permanent contradictory movement within itself. The developing self is in a state similar to that of a chicken which, during its life in the egg, devours its own substance (the white of the egg). Later on, when the male centrifugal force assumes its sexual character, it finds that its "enemy" (the psyche), grown strong because of having fed upon its substance (sexual), has proclaimed itself master of the house. What takes place psychologically is clear enough. The sensibility of the sexual organ has been dulled—whereas eroticism is, on the contrary, highly branched and subtle. Thus sensuality becomes imaginative but does not disrupt the individual's consciousness. Erotically, the man is more like a valley watered by innumerable streams than like a deep gorge where an overwhelming torrent rushes along. Instead of the man being carried away, his mind rules. Sensuality and imagination are at work, but the individual remains "himself". He does not lose consciousness of himself. He cannot possibly lose this awareness during the act of coitus.

Thus we see that man, endowed with his self (which, though static by nature, shelters living seed) must struggle against and overcome the centrifugal sexual movement which tends to lead him into the abyss of the female. Circumcision at eight days helps him powerfully. It gives him the additional dynamism necessary to ensure his escape from the "queen bee" aspect of woman.

Woman. Whereas through all the symbols, allegories and legends concerning YHWH in the Book of Genesis, emphasis is laid on the sublimation of womanhood as a determining factor in human evolution, the covenant between YHWH and Abraham in view of this may well appear as a contradiction; for it aims to dissociate man from the animal species by an operation upon man's flesh only.

It may, however, be noted that, the human psyche being of the same centripetal nature as the feminine sexual function, two contrasting energies to be readjusted do not exist, in womanhood. So woman's problems can and must, psychologically, be dealt with directly. In this field she cannot but respond to Abram's deep and constant wish: "Woman, thou art my sister, my companion." In the truest Hebrew tradition, where the male cannot possibly sink into the primordial female abyss, a psychological and physiological relationship comes into being, thanks to which the woman is given every chance to become supremely intelligent. This is far more real than the projection (in an imaginary heaven) of a mere symbol of the feminine archetype to be worshipped, such as, for instance, Mary, Mother of Jesus.

Social. Centrifugal boys and centripetal girls have different centres of emotional and mental activity, and this well before puberty. Puberty is the result of a slow process of development which has, over a period, been leading the boy outwards and the girl inwards. In this sense it can be said that the emotional and mental life of the child is of the same nature as his sex.

While the development of the self (which is cumulative) finds no opposition in the maturing sexual process of the girl, whose elements are primarily static, with the boy the case is different: there is conflict. As soon as a centrifugal vitality develops in him, it tends to carry the self along with it. Here we see the circumcised and the uncircumcised behaving in opposite ways (with innumerable exceptions). The former does not succeed in ridding himself of the self-consciousness which is well trained to gallop without faltering over moving elements; on the contrary, the latter (the uncircumcised) has the greatest difficulty in not letting himself be carried away by the collective torrent in which his individuality is drowned. He is centrifugal at a moment when his individuation is not assured; and because of that, he risks losing it. It is difficult for him to free himself from his environment and to achieve maturity, because his faculties are conditioned by collective automatisms. He may even go so far as to let himself be swept into some sort of a turbulent current.

We need seek no further for an explanation of the bands of turbulent youths which nowadays are to be found in all countries. Carried away by centrifugal, erotic passion that has drained their emotions as well as their reason, these young people, in love with those who impose themselves on them, carrying emblems, repeating slogans and waving flags, undergo a heroic exaltation which only tears them away from individual egocentricity to topple them into the collective self, which is as functional and "female" as any hive of bees. Their immature freedom breeds a conformity of a kind that tends to regress to a would-be sub-species, where the individual would be in danger of getting lost in a feeling of "belonging".

YHWH is absent from manifestations such as these.

Index of Proper Names

INDEX OF PROPER NAMES

Moses (see also Mosheh), 22, 23, 26, 31, 40, 41, 43, 44, 47, 58, 75, 76, 120, 121, 153, 163, 190, 197, 208, 209

Mosheh (see also Moses), 19, 26, 27, 28, 29, 30, 31, 32, 33, 34, 35, 36, 37, 38

Nadab, 37, 38

Nahhor, 155, 166, 179

Nebuchadnezzar, 40, 41, 167

Nehemiah, 19

Noah (or Noahh), 20, 21, 23, 131, 144, 146, 147, 148, 149, 150, 166

Origen, 45

Pan (the god), 188

Pandera, 208

Peter (or Petros) (see also Simon), 74, 186, 187, 189, 190, 191, 192, 195, 196, 210, 211, 212,

Pharaoh, 22, 23, 24, 26, 29, 39, 156, 161, 165, 189

Philippi (Caesarea of), 180, 188, 196

Pontius Pilate, 76, 194, 206

Ptolemys (the), 44

Qaheen (see also Cain), 64, 134, 136, 137, 138, 140, 141, 142, 143, 144, 147, 150, 189

Rachel, 22, 30, 98, 152, 159, 170, 179, 182

Ram, 19, 20, 163

Rebecca (or Rebekah, or Rivqah), 22, 30, 98, 152, 159, 161, 163, 164, 165, 167, 168, 169, 170, 171, 172, 173, 177

Reuel (see also Jethro), 30, 31, 37

Salome, 210

Samuel, 39

Sarah (or Sarai), 22, 30, 98, 152, 154, 155, 156, 157, 158, 159, 161, 162, 163, 164, 165, 167, 169, 171, 173, 223

Satan, 11, 74, 191, 192, 196, 203, 204, 207, 212

Saul, 39

Sem (or Shem), 21, 149, 150, 152, 153, 154

Set, 135, 143, 144

Shiva, 132

Siegfried, 179

Simeon Bar Yohai, 43, 45, 47

Simon (Judas' father), 202

Simon (Bar-Yona) (see also Peter), 188, 189, 190, 191, 194, 211, 212

Solomon, 39

Symmacus, 45

Tamar, 181

Terah (or Terahh), 21, 154, 155, 166

Thomas (apostle), 210, 211

Titus, 42

Vishnou, 132

Yaaqov (see also Jacob), 170, 171, 172, 173, 177, 178, 180, 181

Yah, 46

Yehoudah (see also Judah), 23

Yeschou (see also Yhshwh and Jesus), 208

Yhshwh (see also Yeschou and Jesus), 59, 70, 125, 131, 185, 187, 188, 189, 194, 197, 205, 207

YHWH (see also Jehovah), 21, 22, 23, 24, 27, 29, 30, 31, 32, 33, 34, 35, 36, 37, 38, 39, 40, 41, 42, 48, 49, 55, 80, 96, 103, 104, 105, 107, 112, 114, 120, 122, 123, 125, 128, 129, 131, 134, 136, 137, 141, 142, 143, 145, 146, 149, 150, 153, 156, 157, 158, 159, 162, 163, 164, 167, 169, 170, 171, 173, 175, 177, 178, 179, 180, 189, 196, 197, 198, 199, 201, 202, 209, 223, 225, 227

Yissav (see also Esau), 170, 171, 173, 178, 181

Yitzhhaq (see also Isaac), 161, 162, 167, 168, 169, 171, 172, 180

Yosseph (see also Joseph, son of Jacob), 22

Zifforah, 31, 32, 33, 35, 37

Zeus, (or Jupiter), 208

CARLO SUARÈS (1892–1976) dedicated a great part of his life to unraveling the revelatory symbolism hidden in the code of the bible. He was born in Egypt and studied at the École des Beaux–Arts in Paris, where he earned a degree in architecture. Between 1927 and 1939, while living partly in France and partly in Egypt, he published a number of books, including *La Nouvelle Creation*, *La Comédie psychologique*, and *Quoi Israël*.

In 1940, while still in Egypt, he considered his writing career finished, and turned to painting. He researched the composition of light, which he expressed by using turquoise blue and rose mauve as the basic colors of his palette. It took him fifteen years of intense work to master his new technique. During this period he wrote *L'Hyperbole chromatique*.

In 1945 Suarès started to write again, and among his more notable works are: *Krishnamurti et L'Unité humaine*, *Critique de la Raison impure*, *La Kabale des Kabales*, *De quelque Apprentis-Sorciers*. Suarès gives us the fruit of forty years' study of the Qabala in *The Resurrection of the Word*, *The Cipher of Genesis*, and *The Song of Songs*.